Praise for *RFPs Suck!*

"This book is a serious keeper. No fluff. No B.S. It's stuffed (as in every pixel on every page) with pointers, recommendations, checklists and whatever else you may need to logically and objectively decide whether to respond to an RFP and, more importantly, how to respond to it.

"If you receive only a single, unsolicited RFP in your career, you need this book to guide you in deciding how to respond to it."

Dave Stein
CEO & Founder
ES Research Group, Inc.

"An RFP can be a wonderful opportunity or a destructive waste of company resources. If you get involved with an RFP, make sure you are in it to win and you know what you are doing. *RFPs Suck!* will help you navigate the RFP world and give you the ammunition to make the best choices (from the start) to grow your business."

Joe Pulizzi
Founder, Junta42
Co-author of *Get Content. Get Customers.*

"Reading this book should be the first step your team takes EVERY time you receive an RFP."

Dan Kemper
President
Schur Packaging Systems, Inc.

"Tom Searcy's *RFPs Suck!* embodies the same enlightened wisdom and insight responsible for helping our company land a project in excess of $50 million. Working with Tom over the years has been one of the more stimulating and rewarding experiences of my professional life. I have come to regard Tom as a close personal friend and can't wait to engage him again."

Richard H. Drennen
President
Superior Mechanical, Inc.

Praise for *Whale Hunting*
By Tom Searcy & Barbara Weaver Smith

"*Whale Hunting* is required reading for anyone who is going after the big fish in a market. Engaging, practical and well-organized, it is simply the best book on major-account selling out there. Someone once said that confidence is going after Moby Dick in a rowboat and bringing the mayonnaise. *Whale Hunting* gives you the tools to pursue big deals with that kind of confidence."

— Keith McFarland
Author of *The Breakthrough Company*: *How Everyday Companies Become Extraordinary Performers*

"I meet with the leaders of thousands of entrepreneurial companies every year from around the world. Every one of them is looking for ways to grow faster, smarter. The straightforward *Whale Hunting* system gives companies a road map for landing the elusive anchor accounts — the big accounts that let them get to the next level of people, services, and revenue. Searcy and Smith have put the key principles together to learn how, with the power of the remarkable story of the Inuit whale hunt. This is an entrepreneur's must-read!"

— Dr. Tom Hill,
Co-author of the bestselling *Chicken Soup for the Entrepreneur's Soul*

"*Whale Hunting* is the type of business book that I wish we saw more of. It has a specific and well-defined purpose — to teach managers how to land really big accounts — and it delivers on that purpose in a clear, practical, convincing and entertaining way. I can tell you that it not only maps well into the big-account sales process, but it also makes for fascinating reading. Simply put, it works."

— **Dave Godes**, *Associate Professor of Business Administration* Harvard University

"Searcy and Smith introduce a nine-phase sales cycle to help small to mid-sized companies accelerate their growth by capturing a 'whale.' *Whale Hunting* shows readers how to create this process and duplicate it again and again. A must-read for anyone who is trying to capture a whale of their own!"

— **Cathy Langham**, *President* Langham Logistics

Praise for "Landing Big Sales with an RFP"

e-book by Tom Searcy

"As a writer of RFPs, I found your well-thought out and documented approach for vendors' consideration to be a great road map. If I was a cheering section, you would hear the roars.

"One of the challenges many consultants (and clients) often encounter is getting longer lead times, for both sides. Time to write and document all the background and requirements, as well as sufficient time for the vendor to prepare their proposal. This, however, is not an excuse for either side to be sloppy or ill-prepared.

"Having said that, it is still amazing to see how many companies' proposals "cut and paste generalizations en mass," use hyperbole throughout, don't justify why they should be selected and don't follow directions.

"I hope that companies take your e-book seriously enough to better manage if and how they respond to RFPs.

"Thanks for the high-value proposition."

— **Gloria Kurant**, *President*
KURANT DIRECT INC.
Strategic Teleservices Consulting

"This is the first e-book I've seen on this grossly overlooked topic and it's definitely a winner. Smaller firms hoping to land large corporate customers will find the most value, but even sellers from big companies will learn some new tricks.

"In short, you'll discover how to qualify, divide and conquer RFPs that make the most sense for your company."

— **Jill Konrath**, *Author, Selling to Big Companies*
Founder, SellingtoBig Companies.com

"Tom Searcy brings truly useful concepts and tools to the sales process — as well as a high-energy, hands-on approach that gets (and keeps) teams fired up.

"The RFP e-book was informative and entertaining, and I've passed it along to several colleagues. Great stuff!"

— **Jennifer Palus**, *Owner*
Palus Business Consulting

"I read your online book about responding to RFPs and found it to be a great compilation! It is rare for us not to get an RFP for a major project in our industry. The good news is that the usual suspects (the industry's consultants) all use their same boilerplate over and over, so we, in turn, regurgitate our previous responses, and off they go. The one main thing from your book that I took to heart is developing a theme to go back to throughout the response. I have never thought about that, but it is a great idea, especially if the prospect knows little or nothing about you."

— **Dan Kemper**, *President*
Schur Packaging Systems, Inc.

"I just wanted to take the time to say that I thought your e-books for RFP and big sales were super.

"I loved the format, content and overall read. You deserve a big high five!"

— **Stephen Shooster**, *Co-CEO*
Global Response

"I was glad to discover that Tom Searcy, founder of Hunt Big Sales, wrote a new free e-book titled 'Landing Big Sales with an RFP' seeing as how his book *Whale Hunting* is on my list of books by successful business people.

"His perspective is definitely that of a successful person and 'Landing Big Sales with an RFP' covers a variety of important topics related to the RFP process."

— **Sam Snyder,** *Founder*
Big Winner

"A THOUSAND *Thank Yous* for writing this e-book. You are SO right.

"How we all wish we could avoid RFPs! However, with your guidance, we will survive and thrive!

"Thank you!"

— **Nancy Hightshoe**, *M.A.*
"The Lady Was a Cop!"

"Outstanding e-book. I will recommend this to my clients. Excellent. Well done."

— **Paul Lanigan**, Owner
Sandler Training
(Ireland)

RFPs Suck!
How to Master the RFP System Once and for All to Win Big Business

Or An All-Inclusive RFP How-to Guide With Samples

and Tips for Writing RFP Responses That Win Government

and Corporate Contracts

Published in the United States by Channel V Books,
a division of Channel V Media, New York, NY.
www.ChannelVBooks.com

Channel V Books and its logo are trademarks of Channel V Media.

amhergris media

Special packaging and distribution rights granted to Ambergris Media

ISBN 978-0-9824739-6-2

Library of Congress Control Number: 2009932284

Library of Congress subject headings:
Requests for proposals (Public contracts)
Contracts for work and labor
Proposal writing for grants.
Proposal writing in public contracting—United States—Handbooks, manuals, etc.
Public contracts—United States—Handbooks, manuals, etc.
Government procurement.

PRINTED IN THE UNITED STATES OF AMERICA

10 9 8 7 6 5 4 3 2 1

First Edition

Contents

III: Write the RFP Response

IV: Evaluate the RFP Response

V: Turning Theory Into Action: Sample RFP Responses With Analyses

Acknowledgements

When my marketing team told me that I should write an e-book on RFPs and offer it to readers for free on my website, I thought they were out of their minds. After all, this was the stuff that my clients were paying me adult money to coach them through. But I knew that arguing would be a losing battle, so, like all other battle-scarred soldiers before me, I raised my white flag, buried my head and jotted down a variety of my favorite RFP-defeating techniques to share with the world.

Thousands of downloads and seemingly hundreds of "Thank You" notes later, I realized that the demand for this type of material was strong and growing. And so I've expanded what was once limited material into what I like to think of as the ultimate guide to conquering RFPs—whether government, private or public—by adding several additional winning techniques and a number of sample RFP responses (with critiques). I also did my due diligence by surveying my audience about the mysteries and troubles they've encountered in their RFP ~~traumas~~ experiences and addressed them here. The resulting book is not something for which I can take full credit.

Thanks go to Wynola Richards for her tireless work on this project, her insights and her sense of humor. To Carajane Moore for handling the many things that could have easily interfered with the undertaking of a new book. To Richard Drennen for his innovative approach to the world of RFPs and our chance to work together. To Dan Kemper's critical eye and nimble mind, and his willingness to apply both to our manuscript. To Dave Stein for his continual support of my work in the RFP arena and for contributing the foreword to this book. And to Jack Burns for always being the voice of reason, balance and practical application.

Thank you to all Hunt Big Sales' RFP clients for your insight into and contributions to this evolving process. Winning RFPs is not only a matter of process but also your companies' past accomplishments and commitment to future growth.

Last but not least, thanks to my marketing and publishing team at Channel V Media and Channel V Books. To Gretel Going for editing and overall management, Cesar Cruz for design and Genna Mazor for promotions. You are all a huge thorn in my side, which is precisely why we work so well together.

Foreword

When I coached sales teams I generally took a tough, often black-and-white, position on responding to blind RFPs. My clients heard me say time and time again, "Follow conventional wisdom: if you didn't write it, your competitor probably did. Let's come up with some more productive ways to spend your time."

Now I'm on the other side of the equation. My company helps its clients write RFPs as part of their evaluation process for selecting sales-training providers. Vendors never influence the content of our RFPs. There is always a budget, a timeframe and executive sponsorship. Furthermore, every vendor receiving the RFP has, at least at the outset, an equal opportunity to win. For those reasons, we expect every vendor to respond—and most of them do.

Needless to say, I have strong opinions about the various nuances characteristic to both sides of the process. But I like to think that whether I'm on the buying or the selling side, I'm consistent in my belief that a good RFP is transparent, rewards thoughtful and honest responses, and is a true means of discerning a vendor's merit based on their ability to meet the customer's business requirements.

I came into contact with Tom Searcy earlier this year when he released his free e-book "Landing Big Sales with an RFP," which is the precursor to the current book. I thought I was pretty tuned into the fragmented sales training industry, so I was surprised that I'd never run into Tom or his company before. And because of this, I was even more surprised by how significant Tom's body of work was. In particular, "Landing Big Sales with an RFP" provided as complete a process as I'd ever seen for evaluating each RFP on its own merit. Not only was Tom's e-book spot on, but he released it at the perfect time: at the height of the recession when everyone was scrambling to identify new approaches and

strategies for finding and winning business. Clearly Tom's approach was to put out his thought leadership for the masses, and I can speak on their behalf when I say that I'm glad he did.

RFPs Suck! is the natural follow up to the e-book. It contains the same signature wisdom and insight, but it offers a clearly delineated process that will undoubtedly help readers across industries, from companies big and small, public or private. This book is a serious keeper. No fluff. No B.S. It's stuffed (as in every pixel on every page) with pointers, recommendations, checklists and whatever else you may need to logically and objectively decide whether to respond to an RFP and, more importantly, *how* to respond to it if you do.

If you receive only a single, unsolicited RFP in your career, you need this book to guide you in deciding how to respond to it.

Dave Stein
CEO & Founder
ES Research Group, Inc.

Introduction

RFPs are a mixed blessing. If you Google "answering RFPs," you'll get 30 articles detailing how awful the whole RFP process is for every one article advising you how to actually deal with it.

It used to be that you could ignore RFPs. Only a small portion of the market used RFPs in their buying process and you could work around those companies. Besides, only the mega-deals required that kind of rigor. Conventional wisdom prevailed and we all felt just a little cocky when we were the incumbents writing the specifications with the client, who was only putting out the RFP because the board required it. We would write our own answers to our own questions and then look over the shoulders of the evaluation group as they used our rubric to score our competitors' responses. We just knew we were going to torpedo past the competition.

Those on the receiving end—who spent weeks slaving over the RFP in hopes of winning the business—had every right to feel bitter. In fact, it was hard not to. RFPs are often designed to favor the incumbent or are nothing more than the buyer's means of gathering free consulting or market research from the participating companies. Because of this, it's not surprising that several organizations have vowed to never answer an RFP again, no matter what.

I suspect it was once an easy promise to keep, considering the complexities and politics of the process, but times have changed. Governance rules dictated by boards and administered by finance through groups like purchasing or procurement have made RFPs and RFQs a dominating component of the large-deal world. So now, not only can you not ignore them, but you don't have access to write the specs for them either (but neither does your competition).

And if the deal has adult money in it, you'd better believe there will be an RFP, an RFQ or another qualifying process that looks amazingly similar. The bottom line is if you don't want to get stuck in the land of little dreams or little deals, you're going to need your 'A' game when handling RFPs.

Even for those of you who are still adamant about avoiding RFPs at all costs, there will inevitably come a day when that irresistible RFP lands on your desk. You know the one: you glance at it and can almost smell the boatloads of money and hear the accolades of your business associates.

"I think we should do this," you'll say to yourself. "Now, who's the best writer we have?"

Sound familiar?

Between the companies I've run and the companies I've helped, I'm sitting on $1.5 billion+ in landed deals through the RFP/RFQ processes. I almost never wrote the specs for the RFP before it went out. Instead, I figured out a system that allows me and my clients to know when we should quit the process with confidence before it even starts, and when we should stay in and kick ass. This book is your best guide on what to know, question and do when faced with an RFP. And it's dedicated to **YOU**, the CEOs, salespeople and all others looking to land big sales.

May you find great success in your undertaking.

Tom Searcy
Founder
Hunt Big Sales

I
Qualify
the RFP

CHAPTER I

The RFP System Is Not Built for You

I f your company is pitching a disproportionately larger client, you go into the RFP process with an unfair disadvantage. It's tough to hear, but it's true:

↦ Many, if not most, Fortune 1000 companies select the provider before they even send out the RFP.

↦ RFPs are not written with small to mid-sized companies in mind.

↦ If you answer RFPs with minimum preparation, your success rate will likely be 7% or lower.

↦ Many RFPs, especially those from purchasing and procurement departments, are a means of seeking the lowest price—and only that.

Companies use RFPs—and increasingly purchasing and procurement—for many reasons that have little to do with the opportunity offered in the official document. Though we all know how expensive and time-consuming the process is to both the buyer and the seller, we go through the process anyway. And though many would like nothing more than a fair system, if you're a small company hunting big sales, the RFP system doesn't offer you that.

Why?

Because big companies benefit from RFPs.

Market Price Strategy.
Companies like to check up on their current suppliers to be sure that what they are paying is the best price available.

Silver Bullet.
"You never know. Maybe there is something amazing out there." RFPs are a way for large companies to get an in-depth look into prices, strategies and ideas from smaller companies with which they are not familiar.

Free Consulting.
RFPs supply information about new technologies, the market, production techniques, materials and everything else connected with the product or service being touted in the RFP. The company issuing the RFP gets all that information, but you likely get nothing in return. (Participating companies take note: don't give away your best ideas.)

Leveraging.
RFPs provide a market price that can be used to negotiate concessions from the current provider.

Accountability.
The Sarbanes-Oxley Act of 2002 demands proof that all publicly-held boards, management and public accounting firms have made the best business decisions in choosing suppliers. Companies don't have to go with the lowest bidder, but they do have to show their reasons for not doing so.

Sometimes a company's board of directors has imposed similar regulations, or a company may have policies governing how suppliers are selected. RFPs are thought to be objective and detailed enough to cover all of those bases.

Despite these obstacles, many companies answer RFPs with outstanding success. So, what are their secrets?

Five Characteristics of Companies That Write Winning RFP Responses

---

1 **Strategy.**
They know their market, their competitors, their strengths and weaknesses, and they know all about the company issuing the RFP. Plus, they have vital strategic plans for their own company. They don't answer RFPs in the dark or write them and just hope that they work.

Can I make this claim for my company?

2 **Time/Effort Commitment.**
They are willing to undertake the following kinds of activities:

    ↦ Assess the RFP and their company as it relates to the RFP

    ↦ Review the cost/benefit ratio of past RFP submissions

    ↦ Assess their chances of success

    ↦ Dedicate large amounts of their employees' time, including the C-level executives and subject matter experts

Will my company and I commit to this time expenditure?

3 **Imagination/Curiosity.**
They are eager to pursue options outside of their normal way of doing business, if necessary and feasible. They'll ask difficult questions and be willing to chase answers by any means possible.

Do I have people in my company who can think creatively and pursue many avenues of exploration?

4 Patience.
They will take as much time as necessary to answer the RFP thoroughly and accurately, with imagination and precision.

Do I have employees who will read and re-read, rewrite and revise our response over a period of weeks or even months?

5 Realistic Stance.
They will say NO to RFPs that don't fit their company's profile for taking on new customers.

Can I depend on people to ask the right questions and know when NOT to respond to an RFP?

If you answered 'no' to any of these questions, you will likely have some difficulty writing a competitive response. It's also worth noting that if the buying process is being dictated by procurement or purchasing, and you don't have access to the end buyers in the process. In this case, you should ONLY answer the RFP if you know you're the lowest cost provider since this is what these departments prioritize.

The good news is that even though the system is not built for you, there are methods that will ensure your success if you decide to respond to an RFP.

Seven Signs of Readiness

Before you even so much as turn on your computer to fill out the RFP's cover sheet, you should decide whether it really makes sense for you to answer this RFP, or if your time and energy would be better spent on a better opportunity.

One important thing to keep in mind is that you're hunting big sales, not little ones. What works in the latter case doesn't work in the former.

Also, that:

↦ Big buyers have big problems and buy big solutions.

↦ Their very "bigness" makes them complex.

↦ Any change they make, like hiring a new vendor, creates ripples that are felt throughout the company.

↦ And most importantly, winning this RFP will have a big effect on *your* company.

Fortunately, there are seven surefire signs that your company is not only ready to answer the RFP, but that it's the right RFP for you to answer. Here are the "7 Signs of Readiness" that your company should consider before answering an RFP:

Seven Signs of Readiness

1 This RFP fits beautifully into our overall strategic plan.
Does this RFP fit into our strategic plan, or are we stretching our plan beyond its borders to accommodate the request?

Think about: Your short-term and long-term goals. If the RFP doesn't fit, don't answer it. If you don't even have a strategic plan, this RFP is not for you. Always determine your company's priorities before you answer an RFP for a big sale.

2 We are capable of working with a company of this size.
Can we adequately perform for this size deal, or will we be swallowed up before the first four months are over? What size is our ideal "big sale?" What is its annual revenue?

Think about: Deciding the size and characteristics of your big sales. If you haven't, then answering this RFP is not a good choice for you at this time.

3 We have the capacity to implement this project properly.
Do we have the resources to execute? Can operations retool in time? Can we add more employees if needed? How about space? Are we promising more than we can realistically deliver?

Think about: Your limitations and reputation. Promising more than you can deliver may earn you the RFP, but failure to deliver will give you a bad (and lasting) reputation in your market place.

11

4 We know the company's entire management team.

Do we know anyone within this buying company? Does anyone in our company know his peers in their company? Does our CEO know their CEO or does our CFO know their CFO? Do we know any former employees? Any board members?

Think about: {
Getting the inside track. If you don't know anyone at the buyer's company nor do you have knowledge of the company, think about skipping this RFP. You won't be able to present yourself to your best advantage.
}

5 We know all of our competitors.

Do we know who our competition will be? How much do we know about them? In which areas are we superior to them? In which areas are they superior to us?

Think about: {
Standing out. If you know nothing about the competition, you have no realistic way to distinguish yourself in your RFP.
}

6 We have all of our corporate ducks in a row.

Is our website pertinent, professional, and up to date?

Think about: Your corporate image. Don't think they won't look at your website. It's the first thing they'll do if you become a potential vendor. Nothing is worse than having your own outdated words, statistics or beliefs come back to haunt you.

Financial History:

Do we know our company's public financial history?

Think about: Your public financial information. Run a Dun & Bradstreet report[1] on your company. If the prospect can access public information about your company's financial history, you should know what it is. Correct any inaccuracies you find.

Organization/Culture:

Have there been any recent changes in leadership in our company? If so, are there factions operating inside our executive team that may affect our success in this sale? Will our entire company be willing to give wholehearted support to hunting this sale? Will we have support from the areas most immediately affected by this RFP?

Think about: How your company is perceived. Major changes in a company's organization can be red flags to the buyer. Anticipate this and answer any questions that might arise throughout your response. Also, don't go into it alone. Make sure you have the support of some, if not all, of the departments and teams that will potentially be working on this account.

---

1 http://www.dnb.com/us/

7 We have a good reputation.

Public Knowledge:
Do I know what is written about my company and me,
and who's saying it?

Think about: ⎰ Listening. Set Google alerts to have all articles containing your company name — or variations on it — sent to you. You should also check blog search engines such as Technorati.com and social media search engines such as search. Twitter.com to pick up anything Google misses. While Google is getting better about this, the "alert" better about this, the "alert" system isn't perfect, so make sure to cover your bases.

Client Assessment:
Do I know what my clients are saying about my company and me?

Think about: ⎰ Asking around. You must know what your customers think and what they'll say if asked. Ask them, "Would you recommend my company and me to others?" Seek Permission to use your clients and your experiences with them in the RFP if relevant.

An RFP can tempt you to consider business that's too big to handle. It can also take you in a direction in which you aren't ready to go, or it may fail to meet other requirements that you've established for considering a new opportunity. Greed and fear that this may be your one shot to "make it big" can get in the way of common sense, but don't give in to either. Be diligent in your assessment of the RFP and honest with your company's readiness.

CHAPTER 3

RFPs to Avoid

Almost always, the RFP itself offers great clues as to whether or not a response can result in success. Don't regard the RFP as sacred material coming from an all-knowing large company or government agency. All RFPs are flawed documents, written by people who are too busy to be writing them. They aren't sure what they want and don't know how to articulate and communicate it in writing.

The good news is that flawed RFPs are often full of warning signs that betray the fact that they're not worth answering. If an RFP contains three or more of the following indicators, skip it. It's not worth it.

1 **No specific objective.**
Try to locate a clear statement of goals. When the buyer's goals or the benefits they seek are unclear, they're likely just trolling for new ideas. If you can't find such a statement, this RFP isn't worth your time. Let this one go.

If you do find such a statement, keep it handy because you'll want to make it part of your central message for the RFP response.

"Watch out" words in an objective:

↦ *Explore*   ↦ *Consider*   ↦ *Examine*   ↦ *Discover*

↦ *Investigate*   ↦ *Perhaps*   ↦ *Probably*

Viable RFPs have a specific beginning and end. They result in an identifiable product or service of some sort. Not there? Just say 'no.' Don't give out free consulting.

2 No money.

Buyers who are given new initiatives from their CEOs or boards will often learn about the market through an RFP process. If the RFP is supporting a new initiative, it is sent out without a budget. Part of the objective of the RFP is to determine the budget.

This is a losing proposition for you. This is a larger company's attempt to benefit from your free consulting and valuable pricing information. Don't do it.

3 Repetitive.

You can tell that the process is haphazard and poorly thought out when the RFP is overly repetitive in its requests. If parts of the RFP don't make any sense at all, then trust me, it's not you; it's the RFP.

The worst offenders are those who have obviously cut-and-pasted their entire RFP together from pre-existing material. If you see the exact same phrasing over and over again, you should make certain not to take on any large projects with this company.

If the RFP isn't worth their time and thought, it shouldn't be worth yours.

4 No access.

When you are denied access to the people who will be using the services or products you sell or to any point of entry, *run,* don't walk, away from this RFP.

Valid buyers want the best deals they can get for their company. They know that the "best deal," however they have defined it, will be the result of give-and-take with a group of people. Therefore they provide the opportunity for that exchange to occur.

Only companies looking for the lowest price or for free consulting won't allow access. They just want to read what you're willing to share with them. Don't put yourself and your company in this situation.

5   Boilerplate.

It's easy to tell a boilerplate RFP process that has been created in response to procurement requirements from one that was created by those genuinely seeking a new supplier.

A boilerplate RFP is written in generalities, not specifics. It reads as if something is just a little *off*. It's obvious that the people writing the boilerplate RFP don't have a deep understanding of the project and, in some cases, lack even a superficial understanding.

Remember what I said earlier: if it doesn't make sense to you, then it's not you; it's the RFP.

Best-Worst Example:
A company attached a letter indicating that respondents should substitute their service offerings wherever they saw the word "products." This company couldn't even be bothered to use the "find" and "replace" commands to identify the services they offer.

6   Too many invitees to the open meeting.

"Y'all come" is a cattle call, not an invitation to a worthwhile open meeting. Unfortunately, too often that's what you'll get. We call that the "shotgun approach"—shoot in every direction and see what you can hit.

Look to partner with companies that outsource whatever it is that you want to bid on as they may have succeeded in breaking the RFP. If outsourcers are invited, it's a completely different ballgame, likely one in which you don't want to participate. (See Chapter 6 for more on open meetings.)

7   A large variety of attendees at the open meeting.

Sesame Street has a song, "One of these things is not like the others." If you can tell that the others don't resemble your company or what you offer in some identifiable way, then you're probably best served by leaving the room. It's obvious the buyers are casting a wide net and don't know exactly what they want.

8 Excessive creative requirements.

Don't give away your best and most creative ideas or deliverables. Requirements of free drawings, sample custom work or the like are yet another guise for free consulting. Don't fall for it.

9 Cycle of request to delivery.

Any RFP response that is required within 7-10 days of your receipt of the request should immediately be discounted. You can be certain that the incumbent knew about the RFP well before 10 days out, as did the company that the prospect favors to win the deal. All you can offer at this point is free consulting.

If you've ever had this happen to you, you know how frustrating and infuriating it is. Too often, people spend day and night working on a proposal and get it in within the deadline, only to find out that the incumbent provider got the deal. It happens time and time again.

Next time, just let it go, and spend the extra time in a hot tub.

10 Tight control of the responses.

When every question in the RFP has tight length restrictions ("200 words or fewer" or "not to exceed one page"), it means the RFP is designed to make the review easier on the reader not to differentiate the respondent.

This restriction doesn't give you the opportunity to fully make a case. Instead, it shows that the buyers are not serious about making a change in providers. They are probably only going through the RFP process so they can prove they have done it. Don't play their game.

11 Rate card request.

The whole purpose of an RFP is to receive a specific proposal on a specific piece of business. This includes all of the elements of people, planning, execution and pricing around that piece of work. If you are being asked for a standardized pricing schedule, this is indicative of a market survey not a business proposal.

Specificity is the key. If it's not there, it's not worth your effort.

12 No reason to leave.

You should find language in the RFP that reflects the problem the prospect is trying to fix, including problems created by the current provider. If there is no identifiable problem in the RFP, then there is no motivation for change. In the end the deal will go to the incumbent.

If you are seriously considering any RFP that contains three or more of these indicators, skip it. It's not worth your time or effort.

The Ten Dumbest RFP Questions We've Ever Seen

1   Detail your company's history. Do not exceed 100 words.

2   Show how your expenditures relate to your stated objectives with regard to the recent change in Policy 534A governing travel. Policy 534A is pending and not available at this time.

3   List all board members for the past 10 years, alive or deceased. Give current home addresses and phone numbers.

4   Estimate the ages of your expected audience members. Give accurate numbers.

5   *From a mandated online application:* Be certain your manuscript is neat and does not contain typos, white-outs or crossed-out words.

6   Using New York City as your conceptual base, list the characteristics of the population. Be specific.

7   If you were a member of the review team, how would you rate your proposal? Poor, fair, good, above average or excellent?

8   In reference to the above-named indicators, are your competitors greatly influenced by sex? Could they be? Be specific.

9   We realize that the possible fluctuations in this scenario are infinite: name them.

10 Accuracy is a vital element of this proposal. To aid in our review, list all errors made with accompanying page numbers.

CHAPTER 4

How Do I
Get in the Game?

Maybe you're sitting there thinking, "Avoid RFPs? What is he talking about? I can't even figure out how to get invited to answer an RFP!"

This is a common scenario. Many small to mid-sized companies either 1) don't get invited to respond to many RFPs, 2) don't receive RFPs until it's too late to answer them, or 3) only receive RFPs that are completely wrong for them. What do you have to do to receive RFPs from companies that make sense for your business? And, importantly, how can you receive them with enough lead time to provide a competitive response?

My best advice is to be a rock in the river. In other words, position yourself in front of the flow of the money. If it sounds logical and obvious (and maybe even a bit corny), that's because it is. You need either to be a provider of the products or services directly requested in the RFP or to be a supplier to the company that was contracted for the RFP. Pieces and parts.

Let's look at some different ways to find RFPs.

Government.

If you're a government contractor or subcontractor (or would like to be), here are a few good places to begin exploring government bids resulting from stimulus funds, grants and everyday government-run projects:

↦ Grants.gov[2] is a "central storehouse for information on over 1,000 grant programs and provides access to approximately $500 billion in annual awards." By exploring the grant requests in this database, you should be able to get a good idea of what projects will be taking place in your industry.

↦ GovernmentBids.com[3] is a source for federal, state and local government bids. The site's researchers track thousands of bid sources daily and offer daily notifications with bids that match the specifications that you provide about your business.

↦ StateandFederalBids.com[4] is a similar database of federal, state and local government bids. Bids found on this site are posted directly by the government.

↦ Onvia.com[5] is a subscription service that monitors government RFPs and sends alerts to its subscribers.

↦ Try conducting an online search for "RFPs" plus the name of your state. This should help you identify opportunities close to home.

---

2 http://www.grants.gov
3 http://www.governmentbids.com

4 http://www.stateandfederalbids.com
5 http://www.onvia.com

Find an Industry Partner.

Join forces with an approved contractor as a subcontractor on a project or program. You will have more credibility as part of a larger entity when answering an RFP, and your company will assume less risk in the process. Be sure to assist in generating the larger RFP response to prove your mettle.

Your Industry:
Any small to mid-sized business that's not already working directly with the government should find itself an experienced, credentialed industry player with whom to build a relationship. Start this process by looking at the current list of 100 Largest Government Contractors. There will be a lot of RFPs and opportunities to bid on in the marketplace, but in the end, familiar faces will usually get most of the money. It's your job to become a familiar face to the government's familiar faces.

Partner with a college or university:
Government grants are a natural meeting point for education (providing the theory) and business (providing the real-work experience). Make yourself well-known to your local college or university. Universities love to write grants but often don't know how to approach those who might be their sub-contractors. So go to them with your proposal.

Here are a couple of university grants I've seen along the way:

↦   A federal grant that went to a state college to build low-income housing. The contractor was the college and the sub-contractor was a local material supplier for the housing.

↦   Several federal and state grants went to schools for technology implementation and upgrades The contractors were the schools and the sub-contractors were the technology providers.

Procurement/Purchasing.

Many companies will turn to a vendor already approved by their procurement and/or purchasing departments. Usually this is a make-the-lowest-bid-and-you-win kind of opportunity. If this is your niche, contact the company and find out about the approved vendor procedure. Then follow it.

It's a good idea to know the procurement and purchasing people in any major company that you consider a target. Begin your communication before any RFPs are under discussion. Talk with the people who will be developing the RFP and see if you and they have any mutual meeting points.

Industry-specific resources:
Every industry has "top 50" or "top 100" listings.[6] These are the companies generating most of the bid lists and RFPs. Get to know the companies that are the best matches for your business, and see that you are put onto their vendor lists so that you receive upcoming RFPs.

Many industries have associations that will track RFPs for you and make you aware of them. You can find out if your industry has such an association by conducting a rudimentary online search.

You might also have luck with sites like The Request for Proposals Database,[7] which acts as a multi-industry hub for available RFPs. There are also industry-centric sites such as Junta42.com and AgencyFinder.com that match companies prior to or in lieu of the RFP process. (The two latter sites serve the marketing and advertising industries, respectively.)

---

6   The 2008 list of 100 Largest Government Contractors is available at
    http://ethisphere.com/government-contractor-top-100
7   http://www.RFPdb.com

Hug a Politician.

Figure out who the most powerful politicians and bureaucrats are in your industry or locale and make friends. Any allocation of funds will undoubtedly be influenced by their relationships and whims, and being in with the "in crowd" will help your chances.

Social Media.

Social media has proved itself not only as a force to be reckoned with but also as one that's here to stay. Many hiring companies are trying their hand at either skipping the RFP process altogether or, at the very least, including social media into its mix of traditional RFP avenues.

Recently, The Current Network, the fastest-growing cable TV network in history (founded by Al Gore and Joel Hyatt in 2004), put out a "TwitteRFP" on Twitter.com [8] to open up its RFP process to five new advertising agencies. [9]

The TwitteRFP read: "This is a TwitteRFP for The Current Network. Searching for a full service ad agency partner. I have 5 empty slots on the distribution list and am on the hunt for creative agencies who also live social media."

(As of this writing, The Current Network has not selected an ad agency.)

Other companies—sick of calling in the same participants to their RFPs year in and year out—are querying their social networks to identify new contenders. LinkedIn's various professional groups and its "Answers" section are good places to look to identify hidden opportunities.

I have no doubt that such social media-centric variations on the traditional process will continue to be adopted across industries. It's a topic for another book, but if you haven't begun establishing your online presence, now is a good time to start, especially if you're serious about being considered for more RFPs.

---

8   The original tweet from Jordan Kretchmer, former VP of brand at Current, is found at http://twitter.com/Jkretch/status/1596088784

9   The full RFP can be found at https://twerbose.com/t7702

II
Understand
the RFP

CHAPTER 5

It Takes a Village...

After evaluating your readiness and the quality of the RFP, you've decided to take the plunge and answer it. What's the first thing to do?

Assemble your team.

Team members should be those who you trust to "git-er-done." They should have the same strong desire to win as you do, and they should make the decision to wholeheartedly commit to the project.

Anticipate that getting people involved in a lengthy RFP process may be more difficult than you imagine. It's time-consuming work. In order to raise their morale and establish one central goal, make sure to:

↦   Identify and get your team members involved as early in the process as possible. If they are part of the group that decides to respond, they will be more willing to continue to participate, in the RFP response process.

↦   Remind them that the purpose of responding is to gain resources for their areas, as well as the entire company.

↦   Give them all the information you have. Talk about the reasons for disqualifying an RFP and why you are choosing to respond to this one.

↦ Be candid about anticipated changes within the company if/when your response is successful. Accentuate the positive.

↦ Remind them that hunting big sales is not the same as other kinds of hunting. Their expertise is what will make the proposal successful.

↦ Provide some type of reward for their participation —compensation, lightened workload, vacation. Whatever works for your company.

So who belongs on your team? And what do they do?

Let's say your company would like to be a government contractor with subcontractors making parts for the airplanes used on aircraft carriers.

First, analyze what the RFP requires.

↦ Quality control   ↦ Logistics   ↦ Warehousing

↦ Operations   ↦ HR

Add additional people to this list:

↦ A decision maker   ↦ A senior person   ↦ A writer

Your team now has eight members, just about the right number for answering an RFP for a big sale.

What are the roles and responsibilities of these team members?

Who	Role	Responsibilities
Carajane *Quality Control*	Content Provider	Outline/write all sections dealing with strict adherence to government standards.
Don *Logistics*	Content Provider	Outline/write all sections dealing with getting the parts to the government when they are needed, not before or after.
Tricia *Warehousing*	Content Provider	Outline/write all sections dealing with having enough parts available when they're needed.
Jamie *Operations*	Content Provider	Outline/write all sections dealing with manufacturing the parts.
Herb *HR*	Content Provider	Outline/write all sections dealing with hiring and working with subcontractors.

Who	Role	Responsibilities
Tom *VP*	Decision Maker	Make decisions related to the process and content. Know "what to do next."
Jen *CFO*	Overseer of Project & Accounting Issues	Shepherd the project from beginning to end. Oversee assignments and meetings. See that work gets done in timely fashion. Assist with financial issues that arise.
Winnie *Consultant*	Writer	Write and revise drafts and final proposal. Ensure final proposal is clear, concise, consistent, and correct.

Although the above are the primary responsibilities of the members of the team, you may need to assign some additional tasks to them or even enlist some outside help. Some examples:

1 Proofreader for final proposal

2 Fact checker

3 Graphic designer

4 Someone to create "best-case scenario"

5 A devil's advocate to critique the best-case scenario

6 Someone to design financial models

This illustration, of course, is not exhaustive. But a quick rule of thumb is that any area mentioned in the RFP should be represented. After all, it's better to begin with a larger group than you need than to write an incomplete RFP response.

All team members should be part of all discussions involving preparation for the writing of the proposal. Content providers can choose to write their own sections, be interviewed by the writer or outline what they believe to be the correct response for their section. The greater the involvement by all, the stronger your response will be.

CHAPTER 6

Open Meetings:
Opportunity or Trap?

Between the time a prospect issues an RFP and the time RFPs are due, the buyers will often host an open meeting for prospective bidders. Government agencies are typically required to hold such meetings, but many corporations choose to host them as well.

Q Should I attend?

A If you are going to answer the RFP, then someone (or two or three people) from your team should attend the meeting. You'll want to send people who can read the room, recognize the competitors, spot insiders who may not otherwise make themselves known, remember names, interpret roles and power positions, take excellent notes and listen for the real answers not just what you want to hear.

Q How do I prepare?

A Discuss with the members of your team the information you are willing to disclose and what you want to know.

You want to disclose as little as possible while getting as much information as possible from the buyers and your fellow competitors. Resist the urge to seem important. Keep quiet and let your competitors talk.

Gather the following information:

↦ What are the steps in the review process?
How long will it take? Who will be reviewing my
proposal? Who's involved? Is it only procurement,
or are subject matter experts also involved?

↦ Is there an approved budget? If so, what is it?

↦ Who is the end user of the product or service?
How and when can I meet that person, team
or department?

↦ What is meant by _____ in the RFP?

↦ Who is the current provider?

↦ Why does the buyer want to change providers
at this time?

↦ What problem is the buyer trying to solve
through this RFP?

↦ Who is my competition?

Sometimes the open meeting is an open inquiry during which
all bidders can ask questions and receive answers online or via
email. Be careful when participating in this type of open meeting.
Don't ask any questions that will give your competitors clues
about your strategy or an advantage over you.

Q So is the open meeting an opportunity or a trap?

A In general, it's a wonderful opportunity to learn more about the
process, your competition and the problems that the RFP is designed
to resolve. It becomes a trap ONLY if you make it one by speaking too
freely or disclosing too much of your company's information.

CHAPTER 7

Think Like a Big Prospect

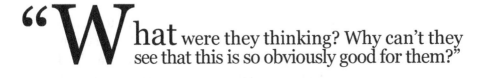

"**W**hat were they thinking? Why can't they see that this is so obviously good for them?"

How many times have you uttered those words after a deal-gone-bad?

Thinking like your buyers is one of the most important ways to prepare for the RFP. If you know only what you want to sell (and nothing about the buyer's needs or criteria) when you are preparing a response, you are not sufficiently armed for the endeavor ahead of you. This is because you'll be responding to the RFP from your point of view, and they'll be reviewing it from theirs. That's one reason why RFP buying decisions often seem so incomprehensible. You and your buyers aren't talking about the same thing.

You've presented your idea—a bright, shiny object that attracts the buyers and even holds their attention for a bit—and their responses reflect genuine enthusiasm. In fact, they're so impressed that the only natural conclusion is that they're ultimately going to buy from you.

Sadly, buying decisions are not based on bright, shiny objects.

They're based on a multitude of thoughts, emotions and conditions that characterize the buyers during the entire process. Buyer groups do not hold one singular thought or emotion throughout the buying process. They respond differently to different stimuli.

Fortunately, there are four different crossroads that can be used as assessment points in understanding what the buyers are thinking.

1 Why do buyers change providers?

Think about the conditions that would cause a buyer to change providers. You know, I know, and the buyers know that changing vendors through an RFP process is a monumental hassle. It takes time, effort and money. Why are they going through it? How does what they are thinking about their current situation shape your response?

2 How do buyers narrow down the field?

What are the criteria that buyers use, but don't discuss, when they select one company for further consideration and eliminate another? You should consider various hypothetical factors in order to decide if this is an opportunity you want to pursue or if it's one that is stacked against you from the start.

3 How do buyers differentiate among competitors?

What are they thinking as they sift through the mounds of data and anecdotal evidence they receive? How can you use those thoughts to your advantage?

4 Decision: Why do buyers buy?

When all is said and done, what makes buyers buy? What are they thinking as they make the final decision? How can you craft a message that answers their unspoken questions?

Let's look at these crossroads together.

CHAPTER 8

Why Do Buyers Change Providers?

Something drastic has happened. A vendor is being replaced.

Large businesses will not make dramatic changes in their vendors unless something has happened. It might be an economic downturn, a merger or acquisition, an internal problem with the current vendor or a new set of governmental regulations. Whatever it is, it leads directly to a change in vendors.

We call this the "Threshold Driver," and it has the following characteristics:

- ↦ It's major.

- ↦ It's essential if a buying decision is going to be made.

- ↦ It expedites the response time.

- ↦ Positive results are expected to take place within a short window of time, sometimes in as few as 60-90 days after it's identified and acted upon.

- ↦ It's not always easy to discover.

Whatever the Threshold Driver is, it causes the buyer pain. Most often, the pain comes from one or more of the following conditions:

Price.
The buyers are looking for lower prices than what the current vendor is charging.

Problems.
The current vendor has caused problems for a department or the company.

Change.
Some shift in leadership, circumstances or focus has occurred inside or outside of the company.

Often times, however, buyers will claim pain they don't feel in order to get some sort of a concession from you.

You want to be able to differentiate between "talking change" and "making change" (or "fake pain" and "real pain"). Don't get faked out by believing that what the buyers say reflects the reality of the situation. After all, if you focus on alleviating a pain that buyers are NOT feeling, you won't be successful in the sale.

Let's take a minute to look at the three conditions—price, problems, and change—through the lens of pain. (Later in this chapter, we'll explore the advantage you can provide when working to alleviate it to set yourself apart from your competitors.)

Pain 1: Price

Buyers always declare price to be a major issue. In today's world, that declaration is not a false one; it's immediate and real.

If price is a pain point for the buyers, you will no doubt see the signs. They often take the shape of:

↦ Stated initiatives to reduce costs appearing in public statements such as annual reports or strategic plans.

↦ Company-wide plans to reduce expenses that result in reorganization, personnel shifts, program review or even talk of mergers.

↦ Specific cuts in budget.

If you don't see these activities, you have no evidence that price is a cause of pain.

If you build your argument around cutting costs—and price isn't the pain your buyers are feeling—you won't win. The current vendor or one of your competitors will match your offer, and you'll have spent a lot of time and money to come in second.

However, if price *is* the pain the buyers are feeling, you'll have to emphasize cutting costs in your proposal. It's unwise, though, to base your entire proposal around this one factor because lower costs provide a threshold that is too easy for competitors to cross.

Pain 2: Problems

Buyers will seek new vendors when the current provider is causing problems. These problems have to be painful disruptions not just annoyances, frustrations or gripes.

When you're trying to determine whether a situation is a problem or an annoyance, look for the real harm being done to the buyer. Don't be misled into thinking that annoyances are actual problems. Annoyances may irritate the buyer, but they don't inflict harm. Problems cause definite harm. Here are a few examples.

Situation	Annoyance	Problem
Money	Frequent billing inconsistencies that are later rectified	Huge overrun that causes negative publicity and slows down the project
Products	Occasional deficiencies	Unusable products or flaws that cause death or major disruption
Time	Late shipments	Delays that stop the project and/or affect other vendors
Behavior	Occasional rowdiness	Sexual harassment, drunkenness, etc.
Contracts	Occasional disagreements over provisions	Not meeting contract specifications

Pain 3: Change

By its very nature, change brings pain to individuals and organizations. Be aware that just looking for a new vendor causes a buyer to feel pain. Even healthy and necessary change can bring about pain as the buyer tries to move forward.

Following are some additional indications of pain-induced change within an organization.

Changes that cause a buyer pain and make it look
for new vendors:

- ↦ New regulations, perhaps requiring objective selection without bias

- ↦ New CEO or other high-level executive

- ↦ Company reorganization

- ↦ New major system such as IT or logistics

- ↦ New product or focus

- ↦ New opportunity

- ↦ Death of a favored vendor

What can I do to ease some of the pain?

Because you're a relatively small to mid-sized company, you can
offer advantages over a large company to alleviate some of the
pain related to price, problems and change:

- ↦ Willingness to negotiate

- ↦ Flexibility to reorganize company structure or operations

- ↦ Innovative solutions

- ↦ Low overhead

- ↦ Accessibility to upper-level management

- ↦ Minimal bureaucracy

- ↦ Quicker response time to emergency issues

- ↦ Greater oversight of individuals

In addition to listing these company attributes (which could likely be used to describe most small to mid-sized companies out there) you should also consider the following seven ideas.

Idea 1:

Show the buyers an 8-14% financial improvement from their current circumstances. This is the Money Threshold.[10]

> ↦   If you show an improvement of less than 8%, you won't meet the general ROI threshold at which a buyer will make a change in vendors. If you show an improvement of more than 14%, the buyer will likely be skeptical of your numbers.

You have to quantify this 8-14% improvement, or it won't be compelling for the buyer.

How do you do this? The following four components of the Money Threshold will help you form your strategy.

Money Threshold

1 Transition and Implementation Costs.
Buyers know that changing vendors costs money. What will be the cost of switching to you as a vendor as opposed to another vendor? You have to quantify the set-up fees, prototypes, tooling, programming, drawings and other items included in your transition. But you also have to consider the "hidden" costs.

Look at the costs of people, business interruptions and errors that will occur during the transition period. Neither you nor the buyer will be at 100% effectiveness. What will be the cost of this phase?

Don't take this figure for granted or leave it up to the buyer to quantify for you. If you do, the buyer will overestimate, and some members at the buyers' table will use the figure to discourage buying from you.

2 Price Differential.

Keep in mind that the buyer will assess all elements of your pricing to determine the "true price" of your proposal. Again, quantify. If you don't, the buyer will. And know that whether you are the lowest or highest in terms of price, you must still quantify the other three components of the Money Threshold.

3 Changing Vendor Costs.

The buyer has undoubtedly put a number on its total costs to retain the problematic vendor, and you should estimate this as well. Of course, that cost is probably high because the buyer is being harmed.

You have to make sure that the cost of your solution — with all of its frustration, fines, fees, business interruptions and other negatives — is lower than what the buyer considers the cost of change to be. Otherwise, you won't get any traction with the buyer.

4 Revenue.

Instead of simply addressing the reduction of costs to a buyer, businesses often present a proposal to increase the buyer's annual revenue. To do so, they might try to impress a buyer by making a statement such as "Your ROI will be 12-22%." This statement is not convincing to a buyer. It takes too much for granted and leaves all the calculation and risk to the buyer. And it's too far into the future.

You'll have to be able to show ROI within 60-90 days as well as over a significant period of time. And you have to show the amortization of the investment over the realized period of return to demonstrate its true value.

Set a conservative return and stick with it, or you'll find the buyer assigning an arbitrary discount to your project out of fear that you overstated its value.

Idea 2:

Remember the old adage "Time is money."

Keep the following principles about time in mind.

Ramp-up time.

"How long will it take for this to be a fully-integrated part of my organization?" If you can provide the buyer with the assistance necessary to shorten and better organize the transition phase (especially as compared to what your competition has proposed), then you will have the advantage.

Time to delivery.

Your project may have one major delivery date or several delivery dates over a certain period of time. Whatever the situation, you have to prove that you can deliver on time and, preferably, ahead of schedule. The most powerful piece of proof you can offer here is a previous success story with a relevant client. Keep a current client list that can be given out at any time.

Executive time spent on the project.

Reassure your buyers that they won't be required to spend excessive time on your project but that they will be kept informed at every step in your process. Also find ways to keep the buyer's current employees from having to unduly disrupt their work during the transition phase.

Idea 3:

Celebrate the status quo. Play up all the areas in which the client will not have to make any changes in order to accommodate your plans.

Idea 4:

Provide a map that illustrates each step you will take through the transition. This step is often ignored by potential vendors who make the incorrect assumption that the buyer knows what needs to be done and how to do it. This is certainly not always the case.

Idea 5:

Clearly define each step in your overall process in terms of the actions to be taken and the people responsible. Also provide a performance threshold for each step. Just be certain that this map reflects what you would normally be doing anyhow and that it is an accurate guide to that process.

Idea 6:

Offer training. Lead the principal individuals who will be affected when you become the provider through a step-by-step orientation. Even better? Offer follow up training after your new systems are in place.

Idea 7:

Develop a procedure for dealing with problems. Specify ahead of time what actions you will take.

The buyer wants to have minimal financial exposure, no negative publicity and very little executive involvement in case problems arise in relation to your deal. In written documents provide assurance that you have a plan to handle unforeseen problems.

Include a clear method for communication with the buyer's executives. You don't get a gold star for resolving conflicts if no one knows you were responsible. You do, however, get credit for conflicts that you handle quickly and judiciously, and without undue buyer executive involvement.

CHAPTER 9

How Do Buyers Narrow Down the Field?

Take a minute to think about the characteristics of *your* current vendors.

↦ What size [vendor] company works best for you?

↦ Do you prefer it if your vendors are based nearby, perhaps in your neighborhood or city?

↦ What value do you place on knowing the person in charge of a vendor company?

↦ If you have a complaint, would you rather speak to the company head or to a department secretary?

↦ Do you pay any attention to your vendors' reputations? Their websites? Their online social media profiles?

↦ Do you prefer to have a formal or informal relationship with your vendors?

The answers to these and other questions establish the framework for how *you* select *your* vendors. Some thoroughly competent providers will not be considered by you because their size is wrong, they're located too far away, their website is terrible, etc. These are all valid, but often unstated, criteria.

Buyers do the same. Their initial criteria may appear in the RFP requirements, but often they don't share everything they're looking for in a new vendor.

The advantage to discovering what unspoken criteria your buyer has for vendors is twofold.

1 It allows you to bow out of the RFP process early if you don't meet some of the basic requirements.

2 It allows you the opportunity to emphasize all the ways that you do meet the criteria if that's the case.

Buyers are looking for function and fit. Buyers want vendors that function in ways that mesh with their company structure and that somehow fit into their concept of the way they run their business.

But how can you possibly know what their idea of a comfortable fit is? And how can you persuade them that you are such a fit if you don't have an opportunity to interact with the buyers?

Use the following tools to do more than read the tea leaves and make some assumptions grounded in practice and reality.

1 Look at patterns.

Identify other vendors the buyer is using or has used in the past. Are there any patterns among them that will help you figure out if your company is a good fit? If you can identify three to five of the buyer's vendors, you will discover some of the following characteristics. (Note: these are only examples and do not represent the totality of characteristics that might apply.)

Possible Criteria Your Buyer Considers When Selecting Vendors:

Size and Annual Revenue.
Some vendors are seen as too small to accommodate the buyer's needs. Others are too big and can't provide the access and feedback that the buyers might like.

Location.
Does the buyer seem to prefer local vendors? This could be because of the need for access, or it might be that the buyer has a strong community presence and tries to direct its money locally.

Financial Stability.
A buyer might prefer a larger company because it can provide more proof of financial stability. Then again, it might prefer start-ups because of their innovation and creativity.

Culture.
Depending on your industry, your culture may have to fit that of the buyer. Do you emphasize your "green" solutions? Do your products appeal to an exclusive minority or to the general public?

Inclusiveness.
Many RFPs are written because of stated initiatives to grow a diversified workforce. When this is the case, it will likely be included within the RFP, but you will not be able to be guided by the buyer's past trends since there likely is no precedent. Obviously you will need to emphasize what you and your company offer in support of this initiative based on your general knowledge of the field.

2 Identify the buyer's preferences.

As you gather information about these other vendors used by the buyer, develop a chart that helps you track your findings.

It might look something like this:

Preferences	Vendor: A	Vendor: B	Vendor: C
Size			
Annual Revenue			
Location			
Financial Stability			
Culture			
Inclusiveness			

If your information is all over the map and you aren't seeing a pattern that relates to any of these preferences, you'll have to dig deeper and define other criteria.

But if you see similar responses across the vendors, you can use these patterns to assess your own company against what you've learned about the buyer's vendors.

Add another column to your chart so that it looks like this:

Preferences	Vendor: A	Vendor: B	Vendor: C	My Company
Size				
Annual Revenue				
Location				
Financial Stability				
Culture				
Inclusiveness				

Fill in your company's information. If your information is notably different from the information of the other vendors, then you are not a good fit for the company.

But if your information is similar to the others, you can proceed with the knowledge that your fit with the company is likely.

3 Do research.

A wealth of information is available online and through social networks. Use business-based networks such as LinkedIn to connect with people in the buyer's organization who can help you find information you need. To start, you'll need to know who the incumbent provider is and what circumstances led the buyer to change vendors.

There are a variety of social networks that can help you connect with people to advance your research.

But Beware:
Open social networks, such as Twitter, might not be the best avenues for conducting research and asking specific or pointed questions since your buyer could potentially be monitoring these communities for feedback on its initiatives.

On the other hand, the buyer might appreciate that you're doing your homework. It's up to you, but I always advise erring on the side of caution when it comes to using social media to gather insider information.

Of course, make sure to research the buyer and the industry online to see if other people have made candid, revealing comments. Disgruntled vendors often express their displeasure online in some capacity. Customers are likely to do the same. It only takes a little time to find out what is really happening behind the scenes.

4 Handicap the preferences.

Not all of the buyer's preferences are going to be equally weighted within your company. Think of this in terms of a sports team — most teams can win on any given day as long as they maximize their strengths and work around their weaknesses. So, while you might not be as big as the companies your buyers traditionally use, you might have extraordinary technological abilities that your competitors don't. Acknowledge the size issue but show how your technology more than makes up for that.

Any time that you spend figuring out your buyer's unstated preferences is time well spent. It will make your RFP responses more productive and help you eliminate those RFPs that don't make sense for your company upfront.

CHAPTER 10

How Do Buyers Differentiate Among Competitors?

What is the buyer thinking about when reviewing RFP responses from you and your competitors?

Buyers are most strongly affected by their desire for consensus and safety. They want to make a decision that will not only be accepted by the entire group, but one that will also be safe. That's because their dominant emotion is fear.

Does that surprise you? You're a small to mid-sized company. How could you possibly scare the buyer? You've just answered your own question! The buyer fears your very smallness.

However, the buyer doesn't always express its fear in those terms. There are many euphemisms for "too small."

10 Ways a Buyer Says "You're Too Small" Without Saying "You're Too Small"

1 You won't have the technology I need.

2 You won't be able to ship parts on time.

3 You'll probably cost more.

4 You don't have enough capacity [money, facilities, people or resources] to handle this deal.

5 You don't have enough experience with this size deal, and I've never heard of you until now.

6 You'll force us to provide extra training for our people.

7 You'll slow down our production time.

8 Your company won't be able to handle emergencies that arise along the way.

9 Your solutions will force my current vendors to change their way of doing things.

10 You'll cause us to have to change our systems [human resources, technological, financial, accounting, etc].

Many times we're so excited about the innovation we're bringing to a deal that we don't take the time to diagnose the possible fears of our buyer. And since we're not addressing what's on the buyer's mind we fail.

Looking at the euphemisms for "You're too small," you can see that they divide into four different kinds of fear:[11]

↦   Fear of change

↦   Fear of conflict

↦   Fear of work

↦   Fear of failure

Let's take a look at each type of fear.

1 Change.

Buyers fear change because it will disrupt "the way we do things here." The whole buying process indicates that changes are being made, so the buyer is nervous from the start. Any innovations that will make the change more severe will be perceived as negatives by the buyer.

You may be suggesting a superior way of doing business—it might be cheaper, more efficient and more manageable—but to the buyer it can seem like too much change and that's scary.

While you're thinking of all of the benefits that will result from your solution, the buyer is thinking of all of the major adjustments being introduced to its culture.

Be very aware that the buying process is by its very nature a scary one for the buyer. It's venturing into the unknown. Your job is to be the one vendor who recognizes this and takes steps to minimize your part in it.

---

11   The "Four Fears" were introduced in the book *WHALE HUNTING: How to Land Big Sales and Transform Your Company* by Tom Searcy & Barbara Weaver Smith, Wiley, 2008.

2 Conflict.

Buyers fear any kind of disruption in existing relationships. The following relationships are involved in any buying situation:

↦   Intra-departmental

↦   Inter-departmental

↦   Buyer and customers

↦   Buyer and current suppliers

We often think of our solutions as being fairly simple. We know that if buyers were to just follow our instructions, they would be in a state of "happily ever after." The buyer, on the other hand, recognizes that living happily ever after is an attainable goal, but also knows of the minefield it has to cross to get there.

Buyer's Fears of Conflict

Intra-departmental	Will employees be eager to accept the new way, or will they dig in their heels and refuse to go along?
	Will they accept retraining, or will they find ways to make the new solution impossible to implement?
Inter-departmental	Will this new way slow down another department, such as accounting, which could then have a huge ripple effect?
	Will the IT department have to carve out time for a major reorganization or for implementing a new technology?

Buyer's Fears of Conflict (continued)

Buyer and customers	Will this solution create an undesirable price differential?
	Will it make an ongoing customer dissatisfied with the services it is receiving?

Current suppliers	Will they get nervous because of this change and begin to look around for other customers instead of fulfilling their obligations to you?
	Will other suppliers have to change they way they're doing business with the buyer to accommodate this program?

---

3 Work.

Buyers do not want to add any additional effort or activity to their people's workload, especially those people who are reviewing the RFP.

↦ What will it take to change the buyer's current methods to the ones you are suggesting?

↦ Will the buyer be forced to hire new people?

↦ How many people will have to be retrained?

↦ How much time will be lost while the program gets underway?

↦ How much executive time will be required?

4 Failure.

When a buyer considers the prospect of failure, it sees itself as part of a gigantic headline in regional or national newspapers. A public failure is the absolute worst kind. Failure means negative publicity, loss of customers, loss of standing in the marketplace, loss of "clout" and loss of personal standing in the community. No buyer wants to be in that situation.

Buyers also don't want to have their decisions questioned by immediate superiors—meaning internal negative publicity—as this could affect promotions, raises and other opportunities.

Assessing a Buyer's Fears

Let's take some time to develop a chart of the buyer's fears. Each situation will draw out different buyer fears, and you want to anticipate these.

Remember: What you consider a big advantage may cause fear in the buyer. Your responsibility is to figure out in advance what that fear will be.

Make a chart that looks like the following in order to assess potential buyer fears that will result from your proposed solution.

Our Advantage	Change for the buyer	Conflict with existing process	Work for the buyer	Failure of our solution
1				
2				
3				
4				
5				

Fill in your core advantages and then assess what fears they might provoke in your buyers.

Following is an example of a completed chart.

NOTE: Your advantages will likely not trigger all four fears.

	Our Advantage	Change
1	"We will reduce your cost year after year."	
2	"We can have your parts on their way one hour after you place your order."	I'm not sure we are equipped to handle such quick delivery. We can't warehouse this.
3	"We can have your project fully implemented at least six months faster than our closest competitor."	

Conflict	Work	Failure
		Can you maintain quality year after year? I'm afraid you can't do this, and we'll lose customers.
We can't ask all our other suppliers to speed up their deliveries, just to keep up with you.		
	That's too quick! We'd have to start now in getting our technology people up to speed and get all the forms we'll need from accounting. We can't spare our people to do all of this work so quickly.	

continued on next page   57

	Our Advantage	Change
4	"We'll reduce your customer complaints by 50% the first year."	
5	"We will fully revolutionize your IT systems."	Well, we can't have that. It's too much change all at once.

Conflict	Work	Failure
		You'd have to prove to me how you can do this. It's been promised and not delivered before.
Will this mean that our IT people will get paid at a higher rate than other departments?	How many other systems will have to change if the IT system changes? What will Edna in Accounting think?	What if it doesn't work? That's too big a risk.

Analyze the solution you will be proposing to the buyer and think of each part that will cause fear in the buyer. Don't think that some are too insignificant to be considered. Put yourself into the buyer's position. What would scare you about you?

So how can you help buyers overcome their fear and move toward favoring your company? Here are some suggestions.

1 Understand their fear and articulate this understanding.
In your RFP response emphasize the many ways that you will make their future easier not more difficult. Decrease the number and severity of changes you suggest. Provide roadmaps to guide the buyer along the path to the future. Don't expect the buyer to fill in the blanks. Explain exactly what the working relationship with you will be like for the buyer. Emphasize the ease with which anticipated changes can be made.

2 Go the extra mile.
Let the buyer know that you will do everything in your power to make the implementation a problem-free zone. Make available the full resources of your company. Provide training as needed.

3 Emphasize what will NOT change.
Make certain the buyer clearly understands which of its many systems will *not* change as a consequence of doing a deal with you. The more you can reassure the buyer that changes will be minimal, the higher your chances of success will be.

4 Use the "Four Fear Fighters." [12]
The buyer undoubtedly likes the idea that it will have leverage in the relationship, as well as access to your company's best and brightest. But it also fears that your company may be too small to deliver. Show the strength of your **people, technology, process, and experience** in your response. This will help the buyer feel comfortable in choosing you.

> **A. People:** Don't just include a pile of mismatched résumés. Create a template for the résumés, no longer than one page each. Include all information you believe the buyer considers important. Use pictures (all the same size) if they help your case. For example, if your buyer is looking for inclusiveness and you have

12 This phrase was coined in the book *WHALE HUNTING: How to Land Big Sales and Transform Your Company* by Tom Searcy & Barbara Weaver Smith, Wiley, 2008.

a diverse staff, pictures will make that argument for you. Don't feel the need to write in complete sentences or paragraphs in the résumés. Your buyers won't be impressed by length. Make lists. In other words, make it very easy for a buyer to read quickly and still catch the important points.

B. Technology: Unfortunately, all you can do in an RFP response is talk about, not demonstrate, your technology. Be clear and concise and emphasize its strength. You'll have an opportunity to demonstrate it and you should (if possible) at the interview.

C. Process: Few things are more reassuring to a buyer than a clearly-defined process. Take the time to tell the buyer exactly how you'll implement this program, citing dates, responsible persons, performance criteria and communication methods.

D. Experience: Don't be shy about talking about your past and current clients or similar deals you have done successfully. (Seek permission from your clients first, of course.) Replicable experience is one of the reasons a big company chooses a big company. In your case, make it a primary reason for a big company to choose you instead.

Four Fear Fighters Chart

Now, for each of the fears you identified earlier, develop a picture of what fear fighter you will use.

Your chart might look like the following.

Our Advantage	Their Fears	Our Fear Fighter
1		
2		
3		
4		

Following is a completed chart.

	Our Advantage	Their Fears	Our Fear Fighter
1	"We will reduce your cost year after year."	**Failure:** Can you maintain quality year after year? I'm afraid you can't do this, and we'll lose customers.	**Technology:** Once we have the system up and running, the costs will decrease each year while we continue to deliver the same results.
2	"We can have your parts on their way one hour after you place your order."	**Change:** I'm not sure we are equipped to handle such quick delivery. We can't warehouse this. **Conflict:** We can't ask all our other suppliers to speed up their deliveries, just to keep up with you.	**Process:** You control delivery day and time, but we can ship parts in as little as one hour if you have an emergency.
3	"We can have your project fully implemented at least six months faster than our closest competitor."	**Work:** We'd have to start now in getting our technology people up to speed and get all the forms we will need from accounting. We can't spare our people to do all this work so quickly.	**People and Process:** We have developed a step-by-step transition map and will provide training for your employees.

Take advantage of every opportunity
to anticipate and alleviate your buyer's fears,
and you and your company will stand
out in the buyer's memory.

Why Do Buyers Buy?

When buyers make buying decisions, they think about risk and performance. So as a potential provider your job is to mitigate their risk and illustrate your performance.

Too often in a proposal, presenters begin with a thorough attempt to make the buyer *understand* the product or service they are trying to sell. So they *educate*. They may spend a lot of time on small details in an endeavor to make the buyer understand exactly how everything works together.

The problem is that buyers don't buy what they understand. You've heard it over and over. "Yes, I understand what you're saying, but gosh, I'm not sure I can ever sell this to *So-and-So*."

So the potential vendor moves on to trying to make the buyers *believe* in the product or service. This time the approach has more passion. "I just want you to believe in what I'm telling you." So they *persuade*.

But buyers don't buy what they believe either. "Yes, I see what you're saying, and I believe it, but *So-and-So* just won't buy it."

What buyers *do* buy is what they can sell and defend later. Because though it's not articulated, your buyer is imagining a conversation that will take place in three months' time, when he or she is being challenged about his/her buying decision.

"Why on earth did you buy XYZ?"

"Why did we change over from the former systems to the new system?"

"Do you have any idea how much trouble this is causing in my department?"

"Do you have any idea how many additional expenses we've taken on as a result of this new vendor?"

Buyers must not only understand and believe what you're selling, but they must also be able to explain why they made the decision to buy. A vendor has to train and equip the buyer with the right tools so s/he can offer an appropriate and useful defense later.

The adage about a picture being worth a thousand words exists for a reason. You can use diagrams and maps to arm your buyer with the information s/he needs. Here are a few examples.

Transition Map.

The transition period is a major worry for buyers. It hits all of their fear points of change, conflict, work and failure. If done poorly transition can be a very clumsy period that sets an uncertain or even hostile tone for the future relationship. Of course, if you have a solid transition map in place — a plan that identifies benchmarks, processes, places to stop and review what has happened and those where you will want to reassess and project what will happen next — it can help guarantee success, not only with this particular deal but with deals in the future.

Project Map.

A clearly-defined project map will alleviate many if not most of the buyer's fears. It will present you as organized and forward-thinking and gives the buyer the reassurance of frequent contact with you, approved communication methods, definite time periods and performance indicators that can be reviewed frequently during transition and implementation.

Schedule and Safety Indicators.

If you have consistently performed on or ahead of schedule in similar projects, you should develop a tool that will let you show this. A chart with a list of comparable projects, scheduled delivery dates and actual delivery dates will work. If, for example, you are a construction company and can also include a large number of days without injury or other delay, that would be useful for your potential buyer to know.

Logistics.

Provide a visual that illustrates your unique logistics system and shows the time spent moving from one step to the next. For instance, your raw materials may be close to your location and easily accessible. If this is the case, play up this distinct advantage which you have over your competitors. Quick delivery of raw materials means faster turnaround for your buyer. Make sure they know this.

When you create tools like these, you give the buyer the chance to step up and say, "Yes, I can tell you why I picked this vendor. Let me show you. Have you ever seen anything so organized and *good for us?*" This is exactly the discussion you want to facilitate.

Naming.
When you develop tools that buyers can use to defend their decisions later, think about naming them. It takes very little time and doesn't have to be alliterative or even cute. When you present a tool without a name, it comes across as an unsubstantial part of your organization's procedures. A name gives the tool weight and suggests a history of use. Even something as simple as "The ACME Method for Smooth Transitions" can add a feeling of importance. Never mind that it was developed yesterday just for this project. It sounds as if it has been part of your company's way of doing business for years. This small step can alleviate a lot of fear.

Add another column to the Four Fear Fighters Chart that lists the tools you will use to illustrate your performance and allay fears.

Our Advantage	Their Fears	Our Fear Fighter	Our Tools
1			
2			
3			
4			

When it is completed, it will probably look something like the following:

Our Advantage	Their Fears	
"We will reduce your cost year after year."	**Failure:** Can you maintain quality year after year? I'm afraid you can't do this, and we'll lose customers.	
"We can have your parts on their way one hour after you place your order."	**Change:** I'm not sure we are equipped to handle such quick delivery. We can't warehouse this.	**Conflict:** We can't ask all our other suppliers to speed up their deliveries just to keep up with you.
"We can have your project fully implemented at least six months sooner than our closest competitor."	**Work:** We'd have to start now in getting our technology people up to speed and get all the forms we will need from accounting. We can't spare our people to do all of this work so quickly.	

Our Fear Fighter	Our Tools
Technology: Once we have the system up and running, the costs will decrease each year.	Technology Demonstration
Process: You control delivery day and time, but we can ship parts in as little as one hour if you have an emergency.	Process Map
People and Process: We have developed a step-by-step transition map and will provide training for your employees.	Transition Map Training Materials

The Bottom Line:
Make the buying decision easy for your buyers by giving them tools they can use to illustrate the high level of your performance.

CHAPTER 12

Learn the Language
Big Prospects Want to Hear

Big buyers listen for a special language and certain key words when they buy. They want to hear how your proposal will impact their Time, Money and Risk.

When writing the RFP response, companies frequently use words that state their advantages but fail to address what buyers believe is valuable. Do the heavy-lifting for your buyer and let them know that you know what's valuable to them. In doing so, you can ensure that nothing is lost in translation.

This advice is particularly pertinent during tough economic times. The game changes considerably, and your language has to change with it. Big companies want their goods and services faster, for less money and with little or no risk.

We may know what words like "quality," "service," "access" and others mean to us, but we don't always know what they mean to the buyer.

So be specific and say what you mean. Just make sure to say it in terms of Time, Money and Risk.

Instead of saying...	Say...		
	Time	**Money**	**Risk**
Quality	"Production lines will not go down because of faulty parts." "You'll never receive fewer customer service calls."	"You'll see repeat purchases and less waste in production."	"You'll have fewer product returns and strengthened investor confidence."
Service	"No delays."	"Few unforeseen costs."	"Happy customers."
Access	"Quick answers."	"Opportunity to negotiate."	"Shared."

Be aware that the buyer will not consider all of your advantages to be positive. Some will produce fear. Take the word "innovation." To you it may be exciting and challenging. To the buyer it may mean uncharted territory in terms of money, time and risk. For example, the buyers may need extra time to ramp up (Time); they may have to hire more people (Money); and they may see the possibility of great failure as well as great success (Risk). Address these issues directly within your proposal.

Simple exercise: When you have completed the first draft of your proposal, read through it and circle every benefit and advantage your company has highlighted for the buyers. Draw a line from that circle to the clear statement you're making about Time, Money or Risk. If you can't connect the circles to the statements, neither can the buyer.

10% Leverage

You design your RFP response to put your company in the best possible light. We all do.

You think of every possible variation on what you're proposing. You emphasize your company's strengths and show your commitment to the project. More than likely, the bulk of your proposal features the following descriptions of your company:

1 History and background

2 Company stability

3 Commitment to the project

4 Belief in your company

5 Basic price structure

6 Emphasis on quality

7 Well-qualified staff

8 Up-to-the-minute technology

9 Flexibility

10 Access to your C-level suite

11 Modern facilities

12 Dedication to customer satisfaction

These descriptions probably constitute about 90% of your proposal and basically answer the questions asked in the RFP.

But what will your competitors say in *their* proposals?

Unfortunately, pretty much the same thing. This 90% in which you and your competitors are similar is no longer unique. It's actually the market standard for your industry. In other words, much of what many companies recognize as their unique value proposition has over time become the minimum standard of performance.

The market standard is what the buyer expects from every potential vendor. It's a solution that is well thought out, logical, doable, financially sound and what all serious contenders will have. It passes the buyer's first test: "Should we seriously consider this vendor?"

But you don't just want to be seriously considered. You want to win. And to do so, you must use the remaining 10% to set yourself apart from your competition. We call this "Framing," or the "90/10 Lens."

The assertion you want to get across in your RFP response is the following:

"Everyone in our industry claims to do X, Y and Z. The fact is that any company answering this RFP for you probably does those things. There are only two or three things that constitute the difference between good and great in our business. They are M, N and O. Only our firm can do M, N and O, which comprise our 10% advantage and result in a 100% difference for you."

Here's how you do it:

1 List all the claims your industry touts. What is the market standard? Make this list as long as you possibly can.

2 List the claims in which your firm is superior.

3 List the claims in which your firm is unique and that truly make the difference in the performance of a provider in your industry. You should have about three of these.

4 Tie these three claims to money, time and risk. This is your 10% leverage and it's a major part of your theme for the RFP response.

Next, take this 10% leverage and turn it into a theme that will be carried throughout your response.

CHAPTER 14

Create Your Theme

NOW that you've found your 10% leverage, you need to construct a theme you can repeat throughout the RFP process.

This theme will define specifically who you are as a company. Don't rely on your mission statement or goals to define this theme. They are usually bland, overly inclusive and easily forgotten.

When answering an RFP, your job is not actually to answer the RFP. It's to sell your 10% leverage, to alleviate the prospect's fears, and to appeal to Time, Money or Risk.

Let me repeat:

When answering an RFP, your job is not actually to answer the RFP. It's to sell your 10% leverage, to alleviate the prospect's fears and to appeal to Time, Money or Risk.

Take a lesson from politicians: regardless of the question, they come back with an answer that reflects their agenda. You have to do the same.

What's your agenda?

1 To sell your 10% leverage.

2 To take away the prospect's fears (using the Four Fear Fighters: People, Process, Technology and Experience).

3 To appeal to Time, Money or Risk because that's what prospects buy.

Remember that in our chronology, you have not yet begun to write the document. Nor should you until you figure out how to craft your story (your theme).

Some suggestions about using a theme in your document:

↦ First, stick to the truth. An RFP is not the place to suggest you are capable of things that you can't actually do.

↦ Second, keep it short and sweet. A sentence or two should work.

↦ Third, insert the "WOW" factor. If you do not have a WOW factor, you probably shouldn't be answering the RFP. Cost reduction year after year is a WOW factor.

↦ Fourth, use care in repeating the theme too often, but DO use it as often as fits with the flow of the proposal.

Because you're stuck with a written response rather than a verbal exchange, your job becomes harder and may take you out of your comfort zone. To address that, we've created a step-by-step guide to creating your theme:

1 Start with your 10% leverage, as explained in the previous chapter. Write it out.

2 Think of the **fears** (change, conflict, work, failure) that this statement could potentially evoke from a prospect. Write them down.

3 Think of ways to tie this statement to **Time, Money and/or Risk**. Write them down.

4 Use these elements to write your theme.

10% Leverage	Fears (Change, Conflict, Work, Failure)
"We can guarantee cost reduction year after year."	**Failure:** Can you maintain quality year after year? I'm afraid you can't do this, and we'll lose customers.
"We can have your parts out the door and on their way one hour after you place your order."	**Change/Conflict:** I'm not sure that we are equipped to handle such quick delivery. We can't warehouse this. And we can't ask all of our other suppliers to speed up their deliveries just to keep up with you.
"We can have your project fully implemented at least six months sooner than our closest competitor."	**Work:** We'd have to start getting our technology people up to speed immediately and get all the forms we'll need from accounting. We can't spare our people to do all of this work so quickly.

Time, Money, Risk			Your Theme
Money: Cost will go down.	**Risk:** Risk may go up.		"Your costs will go down and your quality will be maintained or improved every year. Guaranteed."
Time: Delivery is too quick in some cases.	**Money:** May have to speed up the entire process, which will be expensive.	**Risk:** Will put stress on other suppliers.	"You control delivery day and time. We can ship parts in as little as one hour if needed."
Time: Not enough time to plan adequately.	**Money:** Can't accommodate the quick turnaround.		"Our PTI (Proposal to Implementation) Process includes quick ramp-up, technical training, form templates and easy step-by-step instructions."

Name It and Claim It.

Almost every RFP asks you to explain a process, method, plan or system. "Oh, no," you think. "We don't have such a plan or process."

Yes, you probably do. Similar to the idea of naming your tools, you should also name your processes. Someone in your company knows the process you currently use or what you should use if the need arises. The problem isn't the lack of a process; it's the lack of having formalized the process into something that is written down and clearly communicated.

You must find out what that process is.

Then write it down, name it and pass it around your company. This has a two-fold effect. Your "formal" process will resonate with proposal reviewers, and they will begin to look for similar processes from your competitors. Also, once the process is written down, your company will begin practicing it with more precision than before.

As you write the RFP response, don't feel the need to repeat the exact wording of your theme throughout the RFP. But do work with your writer to find ways to insert the theme into each section. Make it the linchpin that holds the entire proposal together.

CHAPTER 15

Tactics for "Breaking" an RFP

A t some point in the RFP process, you will begin asking yourself the question: Do I have to follow the RFP rules? The answer is "Yes, absolutely," but "No, not really."

RFP systems were not designed to help small(er) companies land big deals from clients much larger than they are. The systems are designed to favor the in-place, bigger, safer provider, NOT YOU.

Then why follow the rules of a system that's designed to eliminate your company? Well, don't. But do be careful. You are allowed to break some of the rules, while others you can only bend. Others you'll have to change later, but only after you have secured the deal.

The rules that you absolutely cannot ignore are the rigid, built-in ones such as proposal length, font size, legibility, submission date, etc. Breaking these rules gives the reviewer a chance to discard your proposal early in the review.

The remaining rules exist as part of a stated process by which many large companies approve new service providers or product vendors. This framework allows the buyer/prospect to get all of the information they need and want from you without offering you much in return.

This process also gives the buyer the ability to:

↦   Avoid making bad decisions

↦   Negotiate below-market-rate contracts

↦   Ensure compliance with the prospect's overall rules and regulations

↦   Protect existing suppliers

In the end the incumbent holds most of the cards. But there's hope. Here are the seven things you can do to "break" an RFP.

Seven Tactics for Breaking an RFP

1   Cast a wider net.
Using social media tools like LinkedIn will allow you to connect with people who can provide you with useful information. Who's the incumbent? Does the company ever change vendors? If so, why? What's the real story behind the RFP? This information will tell you if you have a chance to win or if you should exit the hunt now to save valuable time, money and resources.

2   Get answers any way you can.
We've already discussed the open meeting as a forum for clarifying issues and getting answers. But don't stop with the meeting; push questions through all available channels, including online postings, direct phone calls, emails, face-to-face meetings, etc. As long as you frame your points in a question, you are driving messages and receiving valuable information.

3 Learn everything you can about the incumbent.

Don't be passive about this. Locate people who have previously worked with this provider. Find out his or her business practices. Search for the weaknesses you can use to illustrate your strengths.

4 Be the smartest person in the room.

People who write RFPs often don't fully understand what they want or need. They use the process to generate responses and help them think through what they're looking for. They don't always use the correct language, which is why they often get proposals that don't solve the problems they have.

If you have access to the inside of the company (a prerequisite for hunting a prospect with an RFP), say, "I don't want to interfere with the RFP process, but I do want to suggest that this won't work the way you want it to unless you _____. I'm the expert in this business. I've been doing this for years. I've looked at the RFP and want to talk with you about what I believe you are trying to accomplish. I understand what you are asking for and I know this area better than anyone." Try to create fear that the RFP will not get the result they're looking for.

5 Direct the language and change the understanding of success.

Get them to agree that the language of the RFP doesn't adequately describe what they really want. Then get them to adopt language that is not currently part of the RFP. This assures that when the RFPs come in, yours will be the only one with the new language. In other words, it will be the only one that really discusses what the prospect needs.

6 Explain your reasons for not participating in the process.

If you received the RFP directly from the buyer, it is obvious they want a proposal from you. Should you choose not to respond, take the time to meet with your contact in the company and explain exactly what is wrong with the proposal. Say, "No, I won't answer this RFP unless..." Be sure to do this just after you receive the proposal in case you change your mind after your meeting—this way you will still have time to complete the RFP.

7 **Seek forgiveness rather than permission.**
Many of your competitors — most specifically, the incumbent — are not following the rules as described. Think about where he is while you are in the bid process:

    ↦   He's in the building.

    ↦   He's interacting daily with members of the buyers' table while you're kept at arm's length.

    ↦   He's doing the work you're bidding on.

These tactics are designed to provide you access to two things that are critical in any buying process: information and people. The incumbent already has access to both, which puts the odds in his favor. Use these tactics to either level the playing field or walk away.

If you hit a wall or receive a reprimand for going around the process, apologize and back up. Just remember that you will be committing money, time and effort to your response, and it's your job to make certain that the RFP is right for your company and to put together the best response possible.

III *Write* the RFP Response

CHAPTER 16

Organizing and Writing the RFP Response

The process of organizing and writing the RFP response begins as soon as you decide to respond. Don't wait until the last minute to begin writing. If you do, you won't have the time necessary to do it right.

Let's take a look at the whole process. This timeline begins from the time you decide to respond until you deliver the final proposal.

"We're going to respond. Now what?"

1 Find the **due date and time**, and put both into your calendar.

2 Decide on a **delivery method** — mail, in person or online. Do this early. Some methods are much more complicated than others.

3 Create a **calendar**, working backward from the due date, to establish when each step of the process must be completed. Make calendars for all team members, defining each one's responsibilities and highlighting deadlines.

4 Develop a **method for collecting materials**. I recommend giving the writer the materials as they are completed. That way he or she can begin to organize the information and establish the structure of the final document.

Make certain you have all materials to the writer no later than one month before the due date. You wouldn't answer an RFP that didn't give you a couple of months to complete the response, would you?

5 **Make a list of all the RFP's requirements.**

> **Details:**
> Font size, word length, table usage, labeling and number of pages.

> **Content:**
> Exactly what content is required in each section?
> This is extremely important. You must follow
> the content guidelines absolutely and to the letter.
> You cannot leave out any required content or your
> entire proposal will be dropped immediately.

Give these lists to the team members so that the requirements are always in their minds. Also, keep them handy—you'll refer to them over and over throughout the process.

6 Establish a **meeting schedule** for the team. Regular meetings will help you keep track of exactly where you are at all times with regard to what is required from each team member. Don't let meetings become gripe sessions. Make certain they are productive discussions of the subject at hand.

Online applications.

If the prospect offers an online proposal, log in on the day you decide you are going to respond. Online proposals are often **tricky**, so you'll need to work with the forms a number of times before you are proficient with them.

Write imaginary answers and post them to see what happens. Most online applications give you the opportunity to try different things and save your application to complete later. Only when you push the SUBMIT button are you stuck with what you've written. And as a general rule of thumb it's a good thing to get used to the forms.

Personal note:

I used an online application system once that had more than one set of instructions. The RFP said that certain sections had word-count requirements, but when I actually used the online form I discovered that each question in each section also had a word-count restriction. When my word limit had been reached, I was cut off from answering further. I had designed the response around the total words allowable in any given section and had to redo everything at the last minute — because I had waited until the last minute to get online. DON'T FOLLOW MY EXAMPLE HERE.

Get online and practice.

Especially if you're applying to a government agency. While some applications, like the National Science Foundation's, are fairly user-friendly, others, like the Department of Education and Department of Labor's, are not.

7 Make a **list of the RFP score-keeping standards** so you will know how your final proposal will be rated. You can learn a lot from this. Here's an example:

$\mapsto$ 15%   Compliance

$\mapsto$ 10%   Innovation

$\mapsto$ 20%   Organization

$\mapsto$ 10%   Market expertise

$\mapsto$ 40%   Cost reduction

$\mapsto$ 5%   Implementation speed

You can see that cost reduction is the largest category, so your strongest arguments need to be around that topic. Speed is the smallest category, so if speed to implementation is your unique advantage, you won't get far with your proposal unless you also have by far the lowest cost. Frame your discussions and the amount of time you spend on the RFP around the ways the proposal will be rated. Again, if implementation speed is the least emphasized category, don't spend the majority of your time making your case for speed. Even an extremely high rating there will not compensate for lower ratings in other categories.

8 Now that the rules and schedules are foremost in your mind, **begin the actual writing with the cover page (or pages) and the requested addendums**.

Much of what is asked for in these sections is factual or needs signatures. Don't put these sections off. You don't want to have to scurry around at the last moment trying to find the appropriate person to sign the assurances that the government, for instance, wants. These will be sheets involving compliance, equal opportunity, etc. Since the addendums come at the end, it's natural to think, "Oh, I'll do the body first and wait to do the addendums later." If you do that you'll regret it.

Many people, especially those who don't write a lot of RFPs, think that the addendums are optional or "don't really matter." They couldn't be more wrong. Failure to get proper signatures and provide requested addendums will get your entire proposal dropped out of consideration by the first or second person reviewing it.

9 **Structure the body of your proposal** exactly the way the RFP requests. If they want the Executive Summary first put it first.

One method that I've found particularly useful is to use the exact language from the RFP at the beginning of each section. If they tell you what they want in the section, use those words as your starting place. This will help you stay on point.

If the RFP doesn't recommend a certain structure, then use an organizational device that will work for your situation. Some ideas:

↦   Chronology

↦   General to Specific

↦   Point/Counterpoint

↦   Main points first lesser points toward the end

10 Once you have the structure (and the RFP language for its contents), you should decide how you're going to **address the inclusion of your theme within each section.**

If you know that each section will be reviewed by a different person (a common practice), then write a short paragraph right at the beginning that you can use in each section. It will feel repetitive to you, but it won't feel that way to the reviewer.

And, yes, it's that important. Include the theme wherever space allows it. Vary the exact wording but do include it.

If you have taken the time to get the right theme into a few sentences, its brevity will allow it to work in multiple places with minimal adjustment for the given topic. Besides, you're going to make that theme the pivotal argument for everything you write anyway, so it should fit easily into whichever point you are addressing.

Sample theme that can be repeated in each section
(65 words)

Theme:
Management skills, high quality, low costs, low lead-time.

Fear:
Failure. Can this company manage subcontractors?

Time, Money, Risk:
Less time, less money, less risk

"Our goal as primary vendor is to manage our portion of the contract, providing parts of the highest quality, at the lowest lead-time and lowest cost. For 40 years, we have been a leading supplier that manufactures precise, exact parts with delivery weeks faster than our competitors. This experience has given us the knowledge and competence to manage suppliers, to assure high-quality merchandise and to keep costs low."

---

11 **Be certain you understand** every word others have given to you. If you don't understand any language or terms, then you cannot explain them convincingly. It's a common tendency to accept what others have written without comment, but don't fall into that trap. It is lazy and it will weaken an otherwise strong response.

The writer's job is to bring together different kinds of materials, perhaps written by many different people and add coherence, conciseness and consistency to the entire proposal.

The writer, whether you or one of your team members, will have to rewrite portions to eliminate repetition, clarify terms and promote narrative flow.

> **NOTE:**
> Always take any revised passages back to the original writers to make sure you haven't trampled their meaning in your revisions. The job of writing is back and forth. Everybody needs an editor — rarely does anyone write something perfectly the first time. Expect to spend weeks in the writing process. You should revise as many times as it takes.

12 Write at the 8th-grade level.

Every RFP ever written has jargon and hyperbole in it. Other than those occasions in which you want to quote parts of the RFP, don't use these tactics. Write in simple and clear sentences.

Remember that responding to an RFP is not first and foremost a writing exercise. It is an argument in which you anticipate the reader's objections and alleviate them immediately. The basis of your argument is your theme; everything else supports that argument.

13 Follow practices of clear, concise writing.

↦ The voice of the proposal should be pleasant and strong.

↦ Use the active voice, not the passive.

↦ Make the tone business-like and professional.

↦ Don't use slang or attempt to be humorous.

↦ Avoid using long paragraphs.

↦ Use simple sentences.

↦ Do not refer without explanation to anything not in the proposal. Your RFP response has to be self-contained.

↦ Use correct grammar: no run-on or fragmented sentences, agreement issues or other basic grammatical errors.

↦ Check and double-check your spelling.

↦ Write in the third person.

↦ Never use clichés.

↦ Always keep your audience (the reviewers) in mind. You are writing for *them*.

14 Finally, **give yourself more time than you think necessary to prepare the final proposal**. If you have to print multiple copies, your printer is apt to break down just when you need it most. Have a backup plan.

If you are completing an online application, remember that there could be many, many others trying to get online at the last minute. Perhaps the system cannot accommodate that much traffic. This happened to me once, and the company had to extend the deadline because it didn't have enough bandwidth.

If you are delivering a proposal in person, be sure to get plane tickets, appropriate accommodations, etc. for the person making the delivery. Give them necessary maps to the exact location. Try to anticipate inclement weather conditions and other delaying situations.

Budgets

Budgets require special care and attention. Errors in this part of the proposal probably cause more disqualifications than any other single section.

Be accurate with your mathematics.

Check and double-check every calculation.

Be realistic.

Don't come in so low that you cheat yourself or so high that you'll raise the eyebrows of every reader. Remember: prospects must see an 8-14% improvement in their current circumstances in order to move forward. Improvement of 8% or less is not worth the buyer's time. Promising to improve the situation more than 14%, however, comes across as unbelievable and may be dismissed without serious consideration.

Words and Phrases to Avoid in an RFP Response

Some words are used so often in spoken language that they have no definable meaning when used in writing. Avoid them. If you find yourself using them, grab a dictionary or thesaurus and find more specific alternatives.

↦   **Interesting.** This is the biggest offender. Using it in an RFP will explain nothing at all to the reader. Instead, use a word such as: intriguing, curious, attention-grabbing or plausible.

↦   **Bad, Good, Big, Small, Smart, Dumb.** The range of meanings for each of these words is vast. Therefore, no one meaning is really possible. If you use these words, you're leaving it up to the reviewer to decide the meaning. Not a good idea. Instead, consider words like: imperfect, inferior, honest, superior, massive, enormous, trivial, insignificant, perceptive, insightful, incurious or ill-advised.

↦ **Important.** The reviewer's concept of what is "important" is bound to be different from what you mean to convey. If you want to convey importance, nail it down to describe exactly what the benefit is.

↦ **Probable, Possible.** The meaning conveyed here is "It might or might not happen, and I have no clue if or when." Offer a timeframe.

↦ **Certain.** As an adjective this has no meaning. "A certain business leader said...." It means "I have no idea who said this and maybe I'm making it up." Designate the person by name. If someone is vital enough to quote, then he/she should be named.

↦ **Frequent.** A person's idea of frequency depends on the pleasure or pain he gets from the experience. And that varies by person. Therefore the word means nothing. Again, offer a timeframe.

↦ **Valuable.** This word is severely overused—so much so that it now has no meaning in writing. Use a word or words that specify the extent or meaning of the value.

↦ **Reasonable.** Like many others listed here, the meaning of reasonable is in the mind of the reviewer. So that's how he or she will read your response.

↦ **Quite, Somewhat, a Lot of, a Little Of, Sort of, Kind of.** These words convey nothing and are useless.

↦ **I Think, I Believe.** Wasted space. If you are writing it the reader will assume you think or believe it.

CHAPTER 17

Cover Letter

The two main purposes of the cover letter are to 1) transfer the RFP response to the buyers with official signatures and 2) make a statement of support for the project from the highest levels of your company.

Cover letters may or may not be read; that's hard to predict. I'm a firm believer, however, that you should take advantage of every little chance available to put forward the theme of your response. So find a way to include the theme in this letter.

Though the cover letter is important, keep in mind that it's not as important as other sections, and as such, you should not spend a great deal of time preparing it. Be straightforward and concise. If at all possible keep it to one page. If content is specifically requested include that content.

Be certain to spell correctly the name of the person receiving the cover letter (and proposal).

Following is an example of a cover letter for an RFP that required the following content:

- $\mapsto$ Statement of commitment to project

- $\mapsto$ Qualifications of respondent

- $\mapsto$ Number of employees projected

- $\mapsto$ Financial arrangement requested

The context is a medical outsourcer bidding on staffing within a new hospital. The outsourcer's theme included the following:

- $\mapsto$ Locally owned

- $\mapsto$ Proficiency in data use and control

- $\mapsto$ Merit pay system

- $\mapsto$ Ability to recruit certified physicians

- $\mapsto$ Previous start-up experience

Date
Name of Buyer
Address of Buyer
Address of Buyer
Attention of Specific person

Dear _____:

ABC Company is pleased to submit this proposal for (Name of project and buyer).

Commitment: ABC is absolutely committed to perform the work described in the RFP, if awarded the contract by (Buyer).

Qualifications: ABC has unique qualifications for the (Name of project):

↦   Locally-owned   ↦   Start-up experience
↦   Performance pay based   ↦   Stability and capacity
↦   Successful recruitment model   ↦   Relevant experience
      in challenging areas   elsewhere
↦   Data-driven

Number of Employees:
The initial staffing model will require six full-time physicians. As volume increases, the need for more coverage will be determined via ABC's sophisticated flow analysis using variables decided on mutually by ABC and (Buyer). Our analysis also accounts for variability by day of week and season of year. Coverage beyond the initial physician staffing will most likely be physician assistant and/or nurse practitioner.

Financial Arrangement: ABC requires ($____ per ____) for the start-up phase. After ABC and (Buyer) agree that start-up is complete, ($____ per ____) will be required.

Thank you for your consideration of our proposal.

Sincerely,
Respondent Name
Address
Address
Phone Number
Fax Number
Email address
Website address

Now let's review the letter. Note that it has the following characteristics:

↦ **The theme is upfront and clearly displayed.** Even if the RFP doesn't ask for qualifications in the cover letter, put your theme in anyhow, preferably in the form of a list.

↦ **It's only one page.** This is important. You want everything you say to stand out immediately and at a glance. Whatever you put on a second page will not be read as thoroughly, unless it's a discussion about money.

↦ **It's straightforward and devoid of fluff.** Don't include anything but the basics. Say what you have to say directly.

↦ **It has lots of white space.** Reading can be done quickly and at the same time thoroughly.

↦ **It has only one real paragraph (aside from the money discussion) and it's short.** Readers will read the short paragraph all the way through because it's the only one on the page. And they'll read the paragraph on money because, well, it's about money.

↦ **It contains a list.** Lists are perfectly acceptable in this kind of letter. In fact, they're preferable because of their specificity and brevity.

↦ **The discussion about the number of employees includes a significant illustration** of the technology used by the company and how it can benefit the buyers.

↦ **It includes multiple ways to get in touch with the sender.** It also includes the company's website, so the buyer can get further information. And the address reiterates the fact that it is local.

↦ **It's written in a bullet-point style** with the topic of each division in bold at the beginning.

The cover letter is not the place to explain anything in any detail whatsoever.

You may be uncomfortable putting a dollar amount out there at the very beginning, but you'll have to do it if they request/require it. If you can't fathom putting it there then you should readjust the figure. If the financial arrangement needs a bit more explanation offer it. But don't overdo it.

Take advantage of the cover letter to include your theme, but keep it brief and don't over-explain anything.

CHAPTER 18

Executive Summary

In contrast to cover letters, executive summaries are very important and will be read carefully. Reviewers who are a bit overwhelmed by the sheer number of RFP responses they have to review may choose to concentrate most of their attention on the short executive summary.

But what's an executive summary? Glad you asked.

What it *is*	What it is *not*
A short, concise business case to be read by your executive buyers	A summary of everything in your full proposal
A well-thought out argument stating why the components in your theme make you the best candidate for the project	A laundry list of the first sentence of every paragraph
An opportunity to sell the 10% leverage of your company, alleviate the prospect's fears and appeal to Time, Money or Risk	An opportunity to explain something you couldn't fit in the proposal because of length requirements
A place to take the 90% of your proposal that is market standard off the table and emphasize the 10% where you are superior	A place to list everything you do well

What it *is*	What it is *not*
A forum for you to:	**A forum for you to:**
Write clearly and concisely	Show anger
Be professional	Attempt humor
Get straight to the point	Explain anything in depth
	Write drivel
	Showcase your company

To write an executive summary, go back and collect the data that you have gathered so far in this book:

↦   What is the buyer's pain?

↦   What are the unspoken criteria?

↦   What are the buyer's fears?

↦   What will give the buyer the ammunition to sell and defend later their choice to hire you?

↦   How can you talk about Time, Money and Risk?

↦   What is your 10% leverage?

↦   What is your theme?

The answers to these seven questions go into the executive summary.

Following is a suggested format. I'll continue with the medical outsourcing example I used earlier.

+ **Paragraph #1:** Set up the problem and your solution.

ABC Company is the best qualified company to perform the work outlined in the [Name of RFP].

Our proposal is designed around the following five components:

↦ "We are locally owned and operated."

↦ "Our pay is performance based."

↦ "We have been very successful in recruiting "certified physicians in this area."

↦ "We use technology to make it possible to lower our costs to you."

↦ "We have worked successfully with other start-up hospitals."

+ **Paragraph #2:** Throw your competition under the bus.

"Everyone in our industry claims to do X, Y and Z (list the most pertinent market standards here—i.e. quality and patient satisfaction). Any company that makes it as a finalist for this RFP probably does those things. However, only a few things will make the 10% difference between good and great in this project: local ownership, performance-based pay, successful recruitment of certified physicians, ability to use and control data and previous success with start-up hospitals. Only our firm can make all these claims. That is our 10% advantage that will make a 100% difference."

+ **Paragraph #3:** Local ownership.

+ **Paragraph #4:** Performance-based pay.

+ **Paragraph #5:** Recruitment.

+ **Paragraph #6:** Data.

+ **Paragraph #7:** Start-ups.

In paragraphs 3-7 explain in as few words as possible how your proficiency has a positive impact on Time and Money and decreases the buyer's Risk. Wherever it's appropriate, be sure you alleviate the buyer's pain—and their fears. If recruitment is a special fear of the hospital, include examples of your successes there. If you identified any unspoken criteria you don't meet, emphasize the criteria you *do* meet. Refer to the tools included in your appendix that will help the buyer sell and later defend their choice to hire you.

+ **Paragraph #8:** Concluding statement. A restatement of your introductory paragraph using different words of course.

Work and rework these eight paragraphs until they're as short and powerful as you can make them.

If the RFP sets out certain provisions for what goes into the executive summary, follow them exactly. But make sure you include all the points outlined above, in one form or another. Your explanations won't be as long, but they should still be included.

CHAPTER 19

Final Proposal Checklist

H ere's a final checklist you should refer to before submitting your proposal.

1 Is my theme evident and repeated throughout the proposal? Is it clearly-stated?

2 Have I anticipated and alleviated the prospect's fears?

3 Have I appealed to Time, Money and Risk so the buyers see a reason to buy?

4 Have I followed the structure recommended in the RFP?

5 If no structure was recommended have I used a logical alternative?

6 Have I answered all of the questions posed in the RFP?

7 Is my math correct?

8 Do my responses reflect the RFP's score-keeping system?

9 Does the body of my response read smoothly and coherently?

10 Do I have a method for delivering the response to the correct place at the correct time?

11 Have I double checked for typos? Misspellings? Grammatical errors?

12 Have I included a cover letter and/or executive summary
if required?

13 Have I correctly labeled the pages according
to the RFP instructions?

14 Have I taken all the "Words to Avoid" out of my document?

15 Is the company website up to date and accurate?

	Area of Review	Strong	Average
1	The company's readiness for the RFP response?		
2	The RFP's fit with the company?		
3	Team?		
4	Theme?		
5	Complete, clear and concise answers?		
6	Instructions and protocols followed?		
7	Visually compelling format?		
8	Strong and concise executive summary and cover letter?		
9	8th grade readability?		

Weak	N/A	Comments

IV
Evaluate the RFP Response

CHAPTER 20

How Will My RFP Be Evaluated?

Reviewers are people just like you and me. Reviewing RFPs is a tedious, time-consuming job, and everyone who does it wants to get through it quickly. This isn't to suggest that they don't take it seriously. They do. But if there is any reason at all to disqualify you from the start reviewers will jump on it.

In a typical company the **first person** to see your RFP will check it for the following:

- ✓ Date and time of submission

- ✓ Number of pages

- ✓ Legibility

His primary job—and the primary job of everyone else who will read the RFP—is to find a reason to disallow it. This first reviewer will be looking for the very obvious way in which you did not follow instructions.

I like to think of this first reviewer as **Hector**, a man who wears his glasses low on his nose. He sniffs as he looks at proposals and chuckles out loud when he drops them into the "Disqualified" pile. His job is to find any errors you might have made and he takes pride in doing it.

How to get by Hector:

✓ Follow submission requirements exactly. A minute past the closing time is too late. A few lines over the page requirement will get you disqualified.

✓ Hector can count. Don't try double-numbering pages so you can get that little bit extra in. He'll catch you.

✓ Make sure your finished project is neat and that it looks orderly and well-defined. An illegible proposal cannot be read by anyone, and Hector will not pass it along.

"But this isn't fair," you say. Remember, the entire system is unfair because it isn't built for you. It's built for the prospect. And don't think the supreme value you might bring to a company will make the reviewers overlook the fact you haven't followed their rules about submission, length and legibility. I know for a fact that many people believe value will trump small details. They're wrong. It won't.

The **second person** to look at your submission will compare it with the details of the RFP.

✓ If they mandated a certain form, did you use it?

✓ Did you follow their suggested format?
Font size? Margin size? Does it contain all the required addenda?

✓ Is everything signed that needed a signature?

If the answer to any of the above is NO, then your submission will go no further.

Let's think of this reviewer as **Charlotte**. She does a more in-depth assessment than Hector and it takes her longer—something Hector reminds her of all the time. Charlotte makes little "tsk, tsk" noises as she looks through proposals. She shakes her head a lot. And then she sighs. When Charlotte sighs, your proposal is not going any further.

How to get by Charlotte:

> ✓ Pay special attention to the addenda. They must be completed exactly as instructed, signed by the correct person and put in the requested order.

> ✓ If a form is recommended or even suggested use it.

> ✓ Use the font size and margin that are required. These are big deals to reviewers. Many people submit proposals with smaller fonts or margins so that they can say more. It's Charlotte's job to catch that and she will. And then she will sigh. And you're out.

If you're still in the race after Hector and Charlotte review your RFP response, a **third person** will separate your proposal into all of its different sections. And she'll sort out which section goes to whom. You're now at the stage of review where someone will be reading the substance.

This third person could be **Jill**. Her job is more complicated than it sounds, and it takes even longer than Charlotte's. Jill's primary task is to create a method for comparing your company to all other applicants in terms of size, location, annual revenue and other specific defining elements.

Jill paces when she gets agitated, and she paces a lot while she's reviewing proposals. She tends to study the proposal for a while and then paces around her office or cubicle.

If a spreadsheet form was required and you didn't follow it, she will disqualify your entire proposal because she has no easy way to compare you with others.

Jill will also double-check the other sections in terms of font, margin, structure and other physical requirements. As she passes each section on to a subject matter expert, she has to be certain that all that is required of that person is a review of the substance.

How to get by Jill:

✓ Pay attention to the section of your proposal that offers general information about your company.

✓ If a spreadsheet form is required use it. If not be sure your presentation is logical and clear so it can be easily compared with other companies.

Jill passes on the specific sections to the subject matter experts charged with reviewing them.

The **fourth person** reviewing your proposal may be many people—as many people as there are sections in the RFP. Each section may be reviewed without regard for the rest of the proposal. Keep this in mind as you answer an RFP. To see a sample theme that can be used in each section, look in Chapter 12: "Organizing and Writing the RFP Response."

The subject-matter experts who will be reviewing their individual sections will be judging the following:

✓ Is this feasible?

✓ How does it fit within our current process?

✓ How long will it take to get this up and running?

✓ What will be my role in making this change?

✓ Will this resolve our problem?

If the subject matter expert likes the answers he's getting, he will read and re-read what you've said. And you will have entered into the final phase of review.

But if he begins to think in some of the following ways, it can (and usually does) spell disaster for your proposal:

✓ I don't understand what they're talking about.

✓ This isn't what we asked for.

✓ Their numbers don't add up.

✓ They're promising too much; there's no way they can deliver all of that.

✓ This idea is off the wall.

The final phase will be a meeting of the company's buyers' table. This table will consist of the subject-matter experts reviewing the proposal and representatives from accounting, compliance, IT, HR and any other affected area.

You have no control over what happens at that table, and, even more relevant, you will have no input. But you can anticipate what might be discussed.

✓ How will this proposal fit into the workings of the departments represented here? What will be the impact?

✓ Is it feasible?

✓ Does this resolve the problem we're having, or does it create a new problem?

✓   Does anyone here know this particular company?

✓   How are they regarded?

✓   Is this the best solution for our company at this time?

Individual companies may vary the above procedure, but in general this is how your RFP will be reviewed.

Make a practice of anticipating your buyer's issues and concerns as you are working through your response, and your chances of success will increase.

Top Dos and Don'ts of RFPs

1 **Do** follow the instructions. You'd be amazed at how many people think their value-added proposition is more important than following the exact instructions.

2 **Don't** focus on yourself instead of the client. Remember: the client is interested in you ONLY as you relate to solving the current problem.

3 **Do** focus on the problem that is being resolved by the RFP. Don't just haul out your best argument and forget that it doesn't address the current issue.

4 **Don't** write without a theme or story for your response. Without a theme your proposal never rises above market standards. And to win it will have to.

5 **Do** involve your subject matter experts. Don't expect a winning response written by people who are "good writers" but don't have knowledge of the specific areas.

6 **Don't** expect the reviewers to "just know" information they have no way of knowing. Explain any references that are not part of the proposal.

7 **Do** mention other clients. Give specific examples of what you have achieved. Seek permission from the client before referring to him/her.

8 **Don't** believe the myth that no one is looking at your website anyhow. If you get into the final phase, believe me, they will be all over your website.

9 **Do** get feedback from your clients. If you are preparing a big RFP response, you want to know exactly what your clients will say if asked about you.

10 **Don't** overestimate your capabilities. Every reviewer will be asking, "Is this feasible?"

11 **Do** double-check and triple-check the math in your budget.

12 **Don't** use jargon or "business speak."

13 **Do** remember that your RFP response is an argument not a writing assignment.

14 **Don't** answer every RFP. Be very selective.

V

Turning Theory Into Action:

Sample RFP Responses With Analyses

CHAPTER 21

RFP Review Rubric

NOW that you've taken in more information on RFPs than you ever thought humanly possible, let's take a look at how it can all be applied to some actual RFP responses.

Making use of my various social media platforms, I recently put out a mass request for sample RFP responses — specifically those that weren't successful — in return for a free analysis of the proposal if used in this book. Needless to say, the outpouring of rejected proposals was overwhelming. Not only are there seemingly millions of failed RFP attempts to choose from, there's also a real lack of literature for people to turn to beforehand so they can increase their chances of winning new business through this daunting process.

I chose to analyze seven of these proposals, ones that I thought would offer you the most insight into the mind of the buyer, as well as allow me to illustrate the process outlined in this book with real-life examples.

To give you an idea of what I looked for as I reviewed each response, I've included a rubric that I developed to assist clients throughout their RFP processes. While I've found this rubric especially helpful in reviewing proposals for clients after they are written, I believe that you'll find it an essential way to organize your thoughts throughout the whole process. I suggest keeping some version of this rubric handy so that you can refer to it daily as you work through your proposal. You know and I know that you're going to offer the buyers a comprehensive overview of your products or services. But what this rubric does is continually remind you of all the other areas that cannot be overlooked or neglected. These nine areas will turn your excellent proposal into a winning one.

The Rubric

Name:
Company Name:
RFP Target Company:

Area of Review	Strong	Average	Weak	Comments
1 Your company's readiness for this RFP response				
2 The RFP's fit with your company				
3 Strong and concise cover letter and executive summary				
4 Complete, clear and concise answers				
5 8th grade readability				
6 Instructions/protocols followed				
7 Forceful theme				
8 Alleviate buyer's fears and address buyer's needs				
9 Visually compelling format used to advantage				

Inadequate action or information in any of these areas can mean the end of your proposal. They are NOT listed by importance but only to make for easier discussion in the analysis that follows.

Areas 1-2: Readiness and Fit

Areas 1 and 2 both deal with your company's readiness to respond to the RFP and whether it's a good fit for you. These are not questions the buyer will ask you but questions you must ask yourself. Essentially, is your company suitable for this particular RFP? If you were to win the business, would the buyer even be a good fit for your company? Consider such questions before and as you are writing. You'll know you need to rethink your preparedness if you find yourself saying, thinking or writing statements like the following:

↦ "Although we don't meet this particular requirement, we are confident..."

↦ "We cannot predict at this time whether we will need more personnel to fulfill..."

↦ "Our estimates of time to delivery may not be accurate due to our..."

↦ "We will not be capable of full implementation on your deadline, but..."

These, and other statements like them, all point to a lack of readiness or fit and will mark this RFP as one you should pass on.

Area 3: Cover Letter and Executive Summary

Cover letters and executive summaries are the focus of chapters 17 and 18, respectively. These are both pivotal elements of your response and will be scrutinized by reviewers, so you will need to make an effort to write and review them with great care.

Areas 4-5: Clear Answers and Readability

Areas 4-5 require diligent review after the proposal is written. To be honest, most of the proposals we have reviewed have done very fine jobs in these areas. But never take that for granted. Always review.

Areas 6-9: Instructions Protocol, Theme, Format and Emphasis on the Buyer's Fears and Needs

Areas 6-9 are the final key areas for overview because they will send your comprehensive discussion of your products or services into the stratosphere of winning proposals.

Done well, they will support your response. Done badly, they are, quite simply, deal-breakers.

And the sad truth is these areas are almost never considered when responding to an RFP.

Why is that? People adopt a certain mindset when they begin the RFP process that makes them think:

> ↦ "We only have to answer the questions that they ask."

> ↦ "We are given a certain format and have to follow it."

> ↦ "This is not the place for creative thinking."

> ↦ "This must be a cold, lifeless document containing just the facts."

> ↦ "We have no way of knowing what they *really* want."

All these statements are partially true. That's what makes them so dangerous.

> ↦ You do have to answer what is asked, but you can also **insert other statements** here and there.

↦   You need to find ways to **enhance the format and use it to your advantage**.

↦   Creative thinking is not the main purpose of the proposal but **inserting creativity into your theme and other elements** may be what allows you to win the game.

↦   Even if 95% of your proposal is a recitation of facts, you can still **insert other information strategically.**

↦   Ways exist to **figure out what the buyer wants.**

Sounds good, you're thinking, but how do I do that?

That's what we are going to examine next.

As promised, the remainder of this section will be an analysis of failed proposals along with my suggestions for how they might have been made into winners. I have chosen not to include the proposals in their entirety. I've also sanitized the materials so they cannot be identified specifically, but I tried to include enough information to allow you to understand the context. You'll find that each of these proposals misses the mark because of one or more of the following areas:

↦   **Instructions and protocol were not followed**

↦   **No theme existed**

↦   **No emphasis was put on the buyer's fears and needs**

↦   **Format was not used to the respondent's advantage**

CHAPTER 22

Sample I

A learning management system provider and custom e-course development company is bidding on an RFP from a national association of college and university housing officers for career-enhancing materials for professionals.

SUMMARY:

Positives of proposal:

⟼   Well written

⟼   Excellent use of format to relay information

⟼   Theme given and amplified during the proposal

In many ways this was an excellent proposal, but in one huge way it faltered:

It did not give the buyers what they needed and wanted.

THE RFP:

In paragraph two of the RFP, the buyer described the "Ideal Vendor" in the following statements.

⟼   "Our ideal vendor will act as an e-learning technology and service partner."

⟼   "They will take the time to understand our needs, develop well-conceived and creative solutions and lead us in our design and implementation."

↦ "We are seeking <u>a long-term partnership</u>."

↦ "We desire a vendor/client relationship that will ensure the initiative's future prosperity.

When I read these statements my takeaway is that the buyer wants to work with a vendor that can act as a fully-participating partner. The buyer clearly considers this to be of paramount importance, which is why they spelled out at the very beginning of the RFP.

THE RESPONSE:
Instead of focusing on their ability to meet these needs, the vendor company chose to emphasize its business advantages as its theme:

↦ Expertise in instructional design

↦ Outstanding learning tracking system

↦ High-quality, self-paced product

↦ Customer service

↦ Personal touch

These are all excellent offerings, but every other company that submitted a proposal no doubt emphasized the exact same things. As a result, these characteristics are the lowest common denominator. This proposal simply said, "Me, too."

One exception was the "outstanding learning tracking system," which was proprietary to this company and which they explained thoroughly and with pride. But in reading about this system, one got the impression that few buyer-specific adaptations would be made in the way the system operated. The particular section on the system had a cut-and-paste feel to it as if the name of the buyer company had been put in where another company's name had been before.

Considering the buyer specifically indicated its desire to find a partner, the vendor's emphasis in the proposal should have been on how it would work to do what was best for the buyer. The buyer didn't want a one-size-fits-all solution.

MY SUGGESTIONS:
1 **If the buyer gives clues or states flatly what it wants in an ideal vendor, make that the central focus of your presentation.**
The buyer in this case clearly wanted to be able to read in any response exactly how the prospective vendor would work with them in a <u>mutual relationship</u>. They wanted the proposal to be about them and their needs. They **assumed** that most companies answering their RFP would be able to deliver the services required in high-quality ways. Of course the company needs to know that the vendor is qualified, but more important to them is knowing the exact ways in which the vendor will be involved in and integrated into the process and work.

Presenting an already-established system as the proposal differentiator made the respondents unattractive to the buyer because they couldn't see any way they could influence, change or have a hand in that system, no matter how effective.

2 **Repeat back to the buyers what they want. Don't assume they will figure it out themselves.**
A simple word search turns up the following kinds of information about the respondent's <u>proposal:</u>

> ↦ The respondent only used the word "partner" three times. But the buyer used the word twice in their short original RFP description of the ideal vendor. It may have been important to the buyer, but it wasn't to the vendor.

> ↦ The respondent only used the word "relationship" three times in the proposal.

↦ The term "develop solutions" was not used at all in the proposal.

↦ The term "long term" appeared only in the cover letter.

↦ The buyer was mentioned by name 18 times.

↦ The company writing the proposal was mentioned by name 55 times.

↦ The proprietary tracking system was mentioned by name 75 times.

Clearly, as the reviewers read the proposal, they did not see themselves written into it often enough. Unfortunately, that's exactly what they wanted to see.

And they wanted to read about a partnership or a relationship, not a system that had already been established. They wanted to know the prospective vendor would be flexible, but the proposal doesn't indicate that.

3 Don't go to the effort of writing a proposal if you cannot or will not give the buyers what they want.
This buyer clearly wanted to build a system in partnership with a vendor over the course of the project. The prospective vendor offered an already-established system.

Sometimes, we think we know how to best handle a situation, so we give the buyer a description of that. Instead, we need to determine what they want and give them *that*.

CHAPTER 23

Sample II

> *A consulting company that teaches Capability Maturity Model Integration in software engineering and organizational development through a series of workshops. The company is bidding on an RFP from a larger consulting firm to offer services to its clients.*

SUMMARY:

Positives of proposal:

↦ Clear, straightforward explanation of the respondent's services

↦ Excellent formatting

The company making this proposal was rejected because its costs were too high, or so that's what the buyer told them. The fact that the buyer presented its RFP as a "cost proposal" makes that explanation a handy one, and I suspect it was used widely in the rejection process.

But I think there might be another reason for the rejection:

There was no overall theme. Nothing — except perhaps cost — set this company apart from its competitors.

THE RFP:

This proposal simply answered the command, "Tell us your services and how much they will cost." When buyers ask for that, the implication is that the final decision will be made on cost alone, but that doesn't happen all the time or even most of the time.

THE RESPONSE:

The respondent expressed its entire executive summary in three sentences, slightly sanitized here:

> "The [Buyer] has requested a cost proposal for [short description of consulting services]. As a business focused on helping customers use maturity models to guide improvement, we can provide the requested services.

> "[Vendor] is recognized worldwide as a leader in providing training, consulting and appraisal services."

In essence, the executive summary said, "We're here. We're good. We can do this."

The rest of the proposal simply supported the executive summary. That support was presented in an excellent way; it was thorough and complete.

MY SUGGESTIONS:

1 **Never depend on cost to be the sole determining factor in winning an RFP project.**
You can't expect to win the contract just because you have, or believe you have, the lowest costs.

Buyers don't make decisions based on cost alone, no matter what they say. Other variables enter into the decision. They have to. Your job is to give the buyer the variables that indicate you are the ideal vendor, based on your careful consideration of all issues they've knowingly or unknowingly revealed in the RFP.

2 Learn about the buyer's needs and fears.

Focus on resolving these. Make your proposal about your buyer, not just a recitation of your company's services and attributes. A straightforward presentation of offerings and costs may be just what the buyer requested but to win the project, you have to offer much more.

This company made no claims to being better, different from or even worse than any other company. But surely such differentiators exist. No company that has been in business for more than a decade has done so by offering exactly what other companies in the industry offer. Still, this company did not offer anything that would help the buyer notice it and consider it further.

A well-written proposal has to have a theme — one that moves beyond cost — that relates to the buyer's needs and fears, and the components of that theme must appear early and often throughout the proposal.

CHAPTER 24

Sample III

A web design company is bidding on an RFP to develop
three websites for a large specialty coffee company.

SUMMARY:
Positives of proposal:

↦   Orderly, organized presentation

↦   Strong theme

↦   Good discussion of the buyer's needs

This proposal had many elements that would normally make a
company a strong contender. The buyer ultimately rejected it
because they decided to stay with their existing web designers,
even though they had expressed dissatisfaction with them. This
may or may not be true.

I was, however, able to pinpoint immediately a significant problem
with the proposal:

It didn't use the format to its advantage, and they didn't proof or edit the final copy sufficiently.

For many proposals these oversights would not sink the entire response. But when web designers are maintaining that their writing and designing talents will produce the websites that are the pivotal online presence of any brand, they should be especially concerned with their own presentation. If the proposal is not perfect, how can your buyers have any confidence that you will be meticulous with their websites?

THE RESPONSE:
Following are the first two paragraphs of the vendor's response, with the buyer's name eliminated and some sanitizing and paraphrasing to avoid identification. Otherwise, the sentences appear as written.

"[Buyer] is looking to design and launch three e-commerce websites. To build stronger relationships with its current customers; and to become the leading online source of [specific products].

"With a broad target audience of sophisticated users, the sites must bring to life [the buyer's] brands. Brands based on trust and quality. The sites also need to play an integral role in the marketing strategy of [buyer], especially the offline marketing."

Most buyers would not read beyond these two paragraphs. They would reject it immediately because:

- ↦ There are two incomplete sentences
  (not to mention inappropriate use of a semi-colon)

- ↦ It's wordy

- ↦ It lacks clarity

Incomplete sentences. Although incomplete sentences are used quite often in written materials, they are best avoided in an RFP response, as they can seem inappropriately informal.

In addition, the buyer will notice these sentences immediately because they interrupt the flow of the content. Then the buyer has to conclude:

↦ Your company doesn't understand what full sentences are.

↦ Your company doesn't know it is inappropriate to use incomplete sentences in this context.

↦ Your company cares little about your response and, therefore, will care just as little about the buyer's business.

None of these options are satisfactory. Any of them can only mean one thing: yours is not the company the buyer wants to express its needs to the world via its website(s).

Wordiness and lack of clarity. Everything said here could as easily be said in fewer words with much more clarity. Here's how:

"[Buyer] wishes to design and launch three e-commerce websites to bring to life its trusted and high-quality brands for the following three purposes:

↦ To build stronger relationships with its current customers,

↦ To become the leading on-line source of _____ and

↦ To assist in off-line marketing."

You might be thinking, "Well, that seems awfully petty. Surely, companies wouldn't make a decision based on the first two paragraphs."

Oh, yes, they would. And they do.

MY SUGGESTIONS:

1 **When you're a writer, editor or web designer, or you are in a similar creative position, you must be extremely sensitive to the details of your proposal presentation.**

Any company that works with words or design should expect that they will be held to particularly high standards in these areas. This is, after all, what you do and what you are selling.

2 **If your business revolves around a particular area of expertise your proposal is the place to show your mastery.**
This entire proposal was **text**, something which does not show any design talent at all.

If design is your specialty, use your proposal to showcase it. From the simple use of interesting textual layout and pictures accompanying bios to more complicated design and formatting elements, a web design company should know that there are many ways to demonstrate its skills. This particular proposal, unfortunately, suggested that the vendor is indifferent to the readability or attractiveness of its own important work, which immediately calls into question the attention to detail they would have for their clients' work. By doing so, the respondent made itself an undesirable vendor.

Websites — like RFP responses — must be written with the most selective and impatient audience in mind. Poorly-conceived and executed design, content or interactivity can all lead to failure to connect with the desired audience.

CHAPTER 25

Sample IV

A strategic communications marketing firm is answering an RFP from the state housing authority to assist a city in promoting its work on homelessness, affordable housing and the creation of vibrant neighborhoods.

SUMMARY:

Positives of proposal:

↦ Strong presentation of exactly what was requested in factual form

↦ Good use of format

Despite these positives, there was one area in this proposal that was not executed to the company's advantage.

There was no theme that set the prospective vendor apart from others.

The respondent also misspelled the city's name in the cover letter. That likely wouldn't disqualify the whole proposal, but it would surely be annoying and distracting to the reviewers.

BUT... even with an outstanding theme and no misspellings, this proposal could not win. Read on to find out why.

THE RFP:
Here are the selection criteria given in the RFP:

1 Experience, education or certification   10 points

2 Demonstrate knowledge of the Authority's   5 points
   programs and operations

3 Communication skills, including clarity   15 points
   of proposal

4 Capacity of staff necessary to perform   25 points
   services required

5 Amount of time available to perform services   10 points

6 Creativity of proposal (demonstrate creativity   25 points
   by reflecting your understanding and
   interpretation of instructions in your proposal)

7 Reasonableness and feasibility of your fees   10 points

THE RESPONSE:
While this proposal did have a theme, it wasn't one that could actually set it apart. The theme, loosely translated was: "We know what you need and we can provide it in all the ways that we outline here. We can do everything you need."

More specifically, it said: "Helping you communicate the right message using the right method and the right media at the right price." That's a fine alliterative statement, but unfortunately, it doesn't differentiate the respondent from every other communications marketing firm; it just restates the market standard.

MY SUGGESTIONS:

1 **Always have a theme that sets your company apart from your competition.**
What's needed here is a statement of what this firm can do that can't be done by any other firm. Add to that a statement that explains why what it can do is essential to the efficient, high-quality implementation of the entire project.

These types of statements make a proposal stand out. They elevate it beyond the other proposals the buyer is receiving.

2 **Pay close attention to selection criteria.**
Be aware that selection criteria are very important. Not only do reviewers really follow them, but they can be of enormous help as you write the proposal. Or they can bite you in very unpleasant ways. The selection criteria offered here, however, bite.

If I'm reading it correctly, the two most important parts of this proposal are the capacity of staff necessary to perform services required and, unbelievably, the creativity of the proposal.

Huh?

This is an RFP that lists exactly what it wants you to answer and then bases one quarter of its selection criteria on the creativity of the proposal. This is a perfect Catch-22.

You cannot possibly understand what they mean by creativity. Their explanation is worthless because it doesn't make any sense and probably isn't possible. How does showing your understanding and interpretation of the instructions in any way amount to creativity?

You cannot succeed here. This proposal should have been filed in the trash bin and never pursued. It is not a serious call for new vendors. It's a pro forma exercise either to retain the current vendor or to select a new one the buyer already knows.

No matter how good your proposal is or how well suited this opportunity is for your company, you cannot succeed UNLESS you already have an inside track. For all other proposals, the buyer's response will be, "Well, it lacked creativity." That's 25 points off right away.

Run as fast as you can from any RFP with selection criteria that are such black holes of interpretation and meaning.

CHAPTER 26

Sample V

A group of investment managers is bidding on an RFP from the state judicial retirement system for a U.S. domestic large capitalization equity project.

SUMMARY:

Positives of proposal:

⤇ Well written

⤇ Excellent format

⤇ Solid theme

At first blush this proposal looked excellent. It had all the characteristics that a winning proposal should have, as laid out in the rubric presented in the beginning of this section.

The respondent's theme revolved around a proprietary system that its investment managers use to distinguish between attractive and unattractive stocks. Their intent was presumably that the state government would understand that their system would guarantee stability and growth for the retirement system investments.

The problem is that the managers didn't sell their theme. They simply described it.

THE RFP:
Since this was a government RFP, much of the format was proscribed by specific questions to be answered or situations to be discussed. Within these questions, however, there was leeway for tailored answers.

THE RESPONSE:
In their approach the investment managers exactly described their proprietary system and what it does. Their sentences began with "This system incorporates..." and "This model ranks..." In other words, their entire proposal was some version of the idea, "This is what happens when our system is used."

Nowhere in the proposal was there any evidence for or explanation of why this system is superior to other systems in the industry. The assumption was that the reviewers would "just know" based on all the outlined system capabilities.

Early in the document the managers made the statement that they believe "the key to strong performance is investing in stocks with the right combination of ____ and ____." Then they explained how their system does that. But they never stressed "why" they believe these things. This is a common mistake.

MY SUGGESTIONS:
1 **Remember that your RFP response is a sales document.**
Never assume the reviewers will understand anything that you don't clearly point out.

2 **Never make the "just know" assumption.**
It's not that the reviewers can't or won't recognize excellence when they see it. It's that looking for that evidence is time consuming. Don't make reviewers spend time looking for reasons to hire you — they simply won't take that time. Tell them those reasons up front and often.

3 A proposal is an argument.

Treat it as such. Present your very best argument not just a recitation of the facts.

Know from the beginning exactly what your reviewers need and what you want them to believe/think by the time they reach the end of your proposal. And then lead them to those beliefs and thoughts.

For some reason the format of an RFP proposal makes people behave differently from the way they would in a personal sales meeting. They see the proposal as formal and believe they have little control over their answers. So they write a proposal devoid of passion, assertiveness and essential personal connections. This method does not offer any advantage.

This doesn't mean that you should use exclamation marks or add smiley faces to your comments. But you should certainly make your case in an active, engaging way.

CHAPTER 27

Sample VI

A non profit historical research and consulting firm is bidding on an RFP from the state purchasing department to research, design, fabricate and install an exhibit in the state capitol building. Intended audience: 4th graders and others visitors to the capitol.

SUMMARY:

Positives of proposal:

- ↦ Well written

- ↦ Excellent use of format, including pictures

- ↦ Solid discussion of team qualifications and other exhibits done

- ↦ Excellent identification with the state's history

Once again, we have an excellent proposal that didn't make the cut. Why not?

It lacked a theme to separate it from its competitors.

THE RFP:
The state listed the following objectives for the exhibit to be housed in the state capitol building.

Objectives

      ↦   Connect the public with the capitol through use of information, orientation and interpretive media.

      ↦   Provide specific interpretation that incorporates the 4th grade social studies standards.

      ↦   Provide a self-guided exhibit for visitors.

THE RESPONSE:
This firm rightly picked its people and its previous work as elements to emphasize. But that's all they emphasized.

Imagine a reviewer checking off details as she reads the proposal.

√ Experienced team
√ Knowledge of state history
√ Other exhibits done
? Other

The first three items are the things that every other vendor will no doubt include. The company didn't include anything above and beyond to set itself apart.

MY SUGGESTIONS:
1 **Showcase a theme**.
The firm missed the opportunity to showcase its 10% leverage (see Chapter 13), which is "the 10% of difference (between you and your competitors) that makes 100% of the difference."

Every other organization responding to this RFP no doubt also discussed its past exhibits, its knowledge of state history and its people and their collective experience.

I'm certain the responding firm could have fit additional components into an "other" category to set itself apart. Not only should they have featured such components in the proposal, but they should have integrated these into the theme and throughout the proposal. Sample components could include:

↦ Special flair with lighting?

↦ Dynamic use of colors?

↦ Unusual interactive tools?

↦ Extensive research in one era of state history?

↦ Unique knowledge of available artifacts?

While it's entirely possible that the group reviewing this proposal just didn't like the kinds of exhibits this particular firm had done in the past, the more likely reason the buyer didn't buy is that the response didn't highlight anything exceptional.

2 **Before answering an RFP, you must know what the buyer is looking for**.
Maybe they include that information in their RFP; maybe they don't. Finding that out should be an essential part of any RFP response process. And, if your talents lie in those areas, say so. If they don't, think about not responding to this one.

But don't write proposals that have no theme or that only repeat market standards. Make sure you are selling not just presenting or describing.

Ask yourself, "Why should they pick my firm over everyone else?" Then make that answer your theme.

CHAPTER 28

Sample VII

A public relations and communications firm is bidding on an RFP to manage public relations for a growing software company for one year.

SUMMARY:

Positives of proposal:

⤷ Good use of format with charts, etc.

⤷ Excellent readability

⤷ Great amount of information given

This response, however, had one major identifiable flaw.

It was not answered as described in the instructions.

THE RFP:
The buyer was looking for a public relations plan that would get them through a transition period while they shifted markets and changed their business focus from large companies to midmarket enterprises. They also wanted to emphasize some of their specific capabilities and had recently undergone recent executive changes.

The buyers asked for a one-year plan.

THE RESPONSE:
The firm gave the buyer a proposal for six months. Their rationale was, "We suggest six months because it's harder to look beyond that from our external vantage point at this time."

MY SUGGESTION:
1 **Always follow instructions.**
The buyers asked for a proposal for one entire year. The firm gave them a proposal for six months.

The job of a public relations firm is to look into the future and help companies build a bridge to that future. No, they don't have crystal balls. And, yes, it's hard to look beyond six months. But that's what the buyers asked for. And that's what should have been given to them. For the firm to state they are unable to do that is to say they are not qualified for the job.

It's probable that this firm's proposal was not considered because of that one fact alone.

My final words of RFP wisdom:

Remember: It doesn't matter how great your company is...

RFPs Suck!

om Searcy is a national speaker, author, trusted authority on large-account sales and founder of Hunt Big Sales, a fast-growth sales consultancy and thought-leadership organization. Searcy's primary expertise is working directly with companies and sales teams throughout their big sales "hunts," helping them to compete and win disproportionately large sales in highly competitive markets. His philosophy and process, both of which are documented in his 2008 book *Whale Hunting: How to Land Big Deals and Transform Your Company* (with co-author Barbara Weaver Smith), have resulted in nearly $3 billion in new sales for his company and its clients.

Before entering the national stage, Searcy headed four corporations, each of which he was able to take from annual revenues of less than $15 million to over $100 million—all before he turned 40. Since then, Searcy has helped more than 100 companies grow exponentially with his proven process for fast growth and company-wide transformation.

In *RFPs Suck!,* Searcy shares his rich understanding of the RFP process to help all companies conquer the RFP system and win corporate and government contracts.

For more information, please visit:
www.HuntBigSales.com

For Tom's blog, please visit:
www.HuntingBigSales.com